MW00488291

The BIG CALIFORNIA REPRODUCIBLE Activity Book!

BY CAROLE MARSH

This activity book has material which correlates with the California Content Standards.

At every opportunity, we have tried to relate information to the History and Social Science, English, Science, Math, Civics, Economics, and Computer Technology CCS directives.

For additional information, go to our websites:

www.thecaliforniaexperience.com or **www.gallopade.com**

GALLOPADE INTERNATIONAL

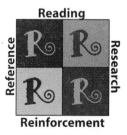

Reading

Reference

Research

Reinforcement

The Big Activity Book Team

Billie Walburn

Michael Marsh

Debra Sims

Michele Yother

Carole Marsh

Bob Longmeyer

William Nesbitt, Jr.

Kathy Zimmer

Jill Sanders

Cranston Davenport

Steven Saint-Laurent

Terry Briggs

Sherry Moss

Cecil Anderson

Chad Beard

Jackie Clayton

Karin Peterson

Wanda Coats

Gallopade is proud to be a member of these educational organizations and associations:

Published by

GALL⬤PADE™
INTERNATIONAL

800-536-2GET
www.gallopade.com

SHOPA MEMBER™
School, Home, & Office Products Association

NSSEA

The California Experience Series

The California Experience! Paperback Book

My First Pocket Guide to California!

The Big California Reproducible Activity Book

The Coolest California Coloring Book!

My First Book About California!

California Jeopardy: Answers & Questions About Our State

California "Jography!": A Fun Run Through Our State

The Califronia Experience! Sticker Pack

The California Experience! Poster/Map

Discover California CD-ROM

California "GEO" Bingo Game

California "HISTO" Bingo Game

A Word From The Author

California is a very special state. Almost everything about California is interesting and fun! It has a remarkable history that helped create the great nation of America. California enjoys an amazing geography of incredible beauty and fascination. The state's people are unique and have accomplished many great things.

This Activity Book is chockful of activities to entice you to learn more about California. While completing mazes, dot-to-dots, word searches, coloring activities, word codes, and other fun-to-do activities, you'll learn about California's history, geography, people, places, animals, legends, and more.

Whether you're sitting in a classroom, stuck inside on a rainy day, or—better yet—sitting in the back seat of a car touring the wonderful state of California, my hope is that you have as much fun using this Activity Book as I did writing it.

Enjoy your California Experience—it's the trip of a lifetime!!

Carole Marsh

Fabulous Flag!

CALIFORNIA REPUBLIC

What does California's motto, *Eureka*, mean?

Hope During The Great Depression!

After the stock market crashed in 1929, many people lost everything during the Great Depression. To make matters worse, a severe drought turned the plains into a "Dust Bowl." As topsoil dried up and blew away, crops could not be grown. Many people fled to California in hope of finding a job. These people were known as Okies or Arkies.

Help this Okie find his way to California.

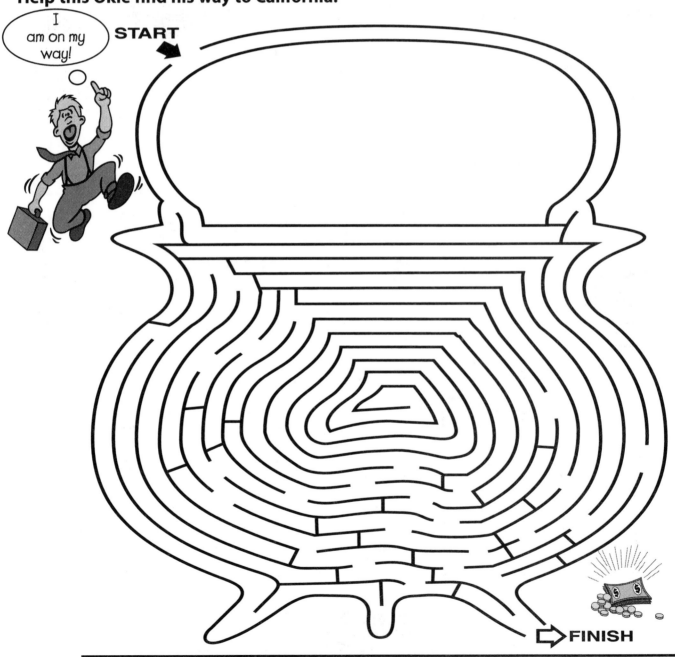

Busy Beaches

California is characterized by its beautiful coastline of bustling beaches.

Find the names of these famous California beaches.

MISSION	LAGUNA	POINT LASALLE
PACIFIC	RED	PISMO
OCEAN	BALBOA	STINSON
VENICE	AGATE	NEWPORT

```
P O I N T L A S A L L E
I R S T V U G K S X Y T
S M O P N B A L B O A T
M K Y A X V T B C B D S
O P S C T N E W P O R T
R K M I S S I O N C B I
R D T F S V R T K E B N
V E N I C E N S M A T S
O K T C V L A G U N A O
S R E D T M R K Y N M N
```

Buzzing Around California

Find the answers to the questions in the maze. Write them on the lines.
Follow a path through the maze to get the bee to the beehive.

California is bordered by the _____ Ocean.

A famous desert in California is _____ _____ .

California is the _____largest state.

_____ is a major Native American tribe in California.

The nickname for Alcatraz Island is _____ _____.

There are approximately _____ rivers in California.

_____ _____ is the highest point in California.

The California _____ is the largest land bird in North America.

California is a very _____ state.

A _____ is an ancient break in the earth's crust.

_____ _____ _____ was California's first highway.

Ships in California

In 1542, Juan Rodriguez Cabrillo, a Portuguese explorer, was the first European to see and explore California. In 1579, English navigator Francis Drake explored the California coast. Also, in 1602, Spanish explorer Sebastian Vizcaino landed in several places along the California coast. Some of the places he visited and named were San Diego, Carmel, and Monterey.

Color the ship in bright colors.

Rhymin' Riddles

I am a state on the West Coast and my name starts with a "C."
In 1849, people looking for gold came to me.

Who am I? _____

I am a historical figure who saw destruction of trees.
There had to be a solution and I found the keys.

Who am I? _____

With the white man we clashed and so we were banished.
Even some of our tribes forever vanished.

Who am I? _____

For the Indians in California, I began a mission. Soon, good will gave way
to suspicion.

Who am I? _____

Solving problems is my game, created in San Francisco brought me fame.

What am I? _____ _____

ANSWERS: California, John Muir, Modoc Indian tribe, Junipero Serra, United Nations

All Around California Crossword Puzzle

California is surrounded by three states and the Pacific Ocean. To find out what they are, fill in the crossword puzzle using the clues below.

1. **A state east of California.** (across)
2. **Where the ocean meets the land in California.** (down)
3. **A country south of California.** (across)
4. **A famous tree in California.** (across)
5. **The capital of California.** (down)
6. **The famous fault line in California.** (down)
7. **A state north of California.** (across)
8. **A state east of California and north of Arizona.** (across)

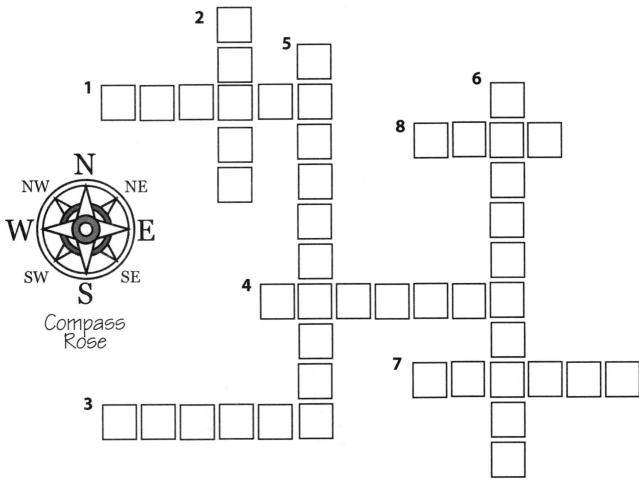

Compass Rose

This Old House

Take yourself back 100 years. Can you imagine what life would be like in the Victorian Era? What did turn-of-the-century Californians have? How did they live? See if you can pick out which of the following items people at the turn of the century had and which ones they did not.

Circle the things you might find or use in your 1900 home.

Chronicling California

Publishing giant, William Randolph Hearst was born to a prosperous family in San Francisco on April 29, 1863. Before dying in 1951, Hearst had accumulated over 25 newspapers, 14 magazines, 11 radio stations, 2 news services, a newsreel company, and a film company. Wow!

Test your publishing skills by writing a newsletter about California. You can write your newsletter on the computer, write it out by hand, or cut and paste words from magazines or other places.

1. Give your newsletter a "catchy name." Make sure your readers know what the newsletter is about.

2. Once you've come up with a name, center it in bold letters at the top of the page. Under the title, you will need a line with the following information: Volume number, date, issue number, and purchase price.

3. Decide what information you want to include in your newsletter about California. Some suggestions might be: exciting travel destinations, highlighting the famous lives of Californians, urgent environmental concerns.

4. Jazz up your newsletter with puzzles, cartoons, trivia tidbits, advice columns, etc. Whatever you decide to write about, have fun!

5. Write some ideas for your newsletter here:

_____

_____

_____

_____

_____

_____

Let's Get Regional

California and the entire Pacific region are rich in many types of natural resources. Lots of sunshine, forests, minerals, rich soil, and plenty of water for irrigation help to make it a great state. It has a year-round growing season! From mining to wine-making or farming to fishing, it is a very productive state!

Listed below are some resources of California. Beside each resource, write in at least one use for each. Write in more than one if you can!

RESOURCE	USES	RESOURCE	USES
COAL	_____	FRUIT	_____
COTTON	_____	GOLD	_____
FORESTS	_____	OIL	_____
FISH	_____	WHEAT	_____

CALIFORNIA IMMIGRATION

Throughout its history as a state, immigrants have been attracted to California in search of a better life. People came from all over the world and, like the ocean, they came in waves. Colonial Mexico provided the first settlers to California. The Spanish settlers tended to settle in the southern part of the new territory because it was near Mexico. By 1849, the state was filled with new immigrants in search of gold.

The second wave of immigrants came from the Midwest during the 1930s and 1940s. Farmers in this region were hit hard by a terrible drought known as the Dust Bowl. Many people came from states such as Oklahoma and Arkansas. They became known as Okies or Arkies.

USE THE RHYMING CLUES TO FILL IN THE BLANKS.

1. People left their land of strife to come to California for a better __ __ __ __.

2. __ __ __ __ __ __ __ colonists left their home, off to California they did roam.

3. Immigrants are people that are very brave and those going to California came in a __ __ __ __.

4. Many immigrants came in search of __ __ __ __.
   In California you'll be rich, they were told.

5. The Okies and __ __ __ __ __ __ fled their dust,
   To California they came, a state they could trust.

An immigrant is a person who migrates to another country in hopes of a better life.

Make a Wampum Necklace

California Indians used wampum (beads made from colored shells and bones) to barter with early settlers. They traded wampum for food and supplies. The Indians sometimes traded wampum for trinkets.

You can make your own wampum necklace using dried macaroni and string. Thread the dried macaroni onto a long piece of string and tie.

Using markers or crayons, color the wampum necklace.

Color the shells.

The Railroads of California

The Central Pacific Railroad was built thanks to the labor of Chinese immigrants who worked hard to build the railroads and were willing to work for lower wages than everyone else. Unfortunately, many people did not like the Chinese and started anti-Chinese groups. Today, Chinese-Americans are an important part of California's delightful diversity.

Help Huang Lan-Ting get to work on the railroad.

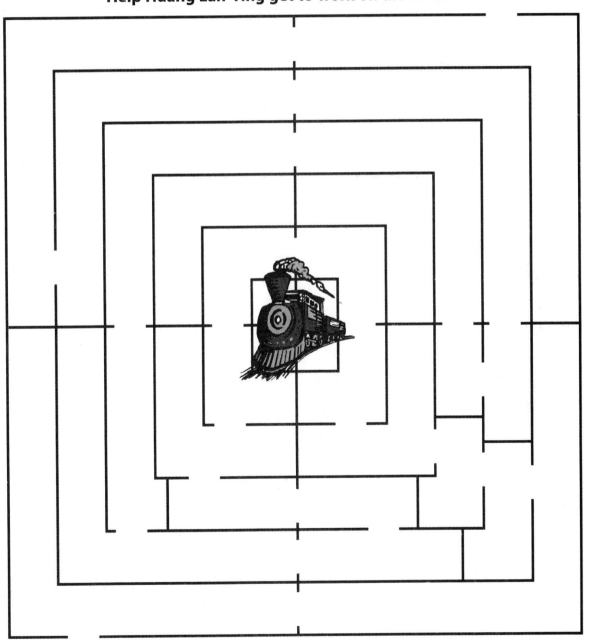

The Goods For The Gold

In 1849, the California Gold Rush was at its peak. Men came from all over the United States, Mexico, South America, Hawaii, Australia, and even Europe to join the search. They were known as "Forty-Niners."

Circle the things the "Forty-Niners" would need.

A Day In The Life Of A "Forty-Niner"

**Pretend you are a miner in the early days of the Gold Rush.
You keep a diary of what you do each day.
Write in the "diary" what you might have done on a typical day.**

California,
The Golden State

Match the name of each California state symbol on the left with its picture on the right.

State Nickname

State Bird

State Motto

State Insect

State Flower

State Tree

State Gem

State Marine Mammal

THE GOLDEN STATE

Eureka!

Farm Country

California is the leading state in agriculture. Twenty-nine percent of California's total land area is farmland. Nearly 70 kinds of fruits, vegetables, and grains are grown here! Overall, 55 percent of all the nation's fruits, vegetables, and nuts are produced in California. Just over 99 percent of these U.S. crops come from California: almonds, walnuts, pistachios, olives, artichokes, clovers, figs, dates, prunes, and raisins. Speaking of raisins, 91 percent of the nation's grape crop comes from California! The lettuce you eat in your salad could very well be from here, too! Seventy-two percent of the nation's lettuce is grown in California. California has a large food-processing industry and is the nation's top exporter of food: 55 percent goes to Pacific Rim countries, 18 pecent to Canada, 9 percent to Europe, and 5 percent to Mexico. Now we understand why California has been the number one farming state for many years in a row!

Using the information in the paragraph above, graph the different items on the bar graph below. The first one has been done for you.

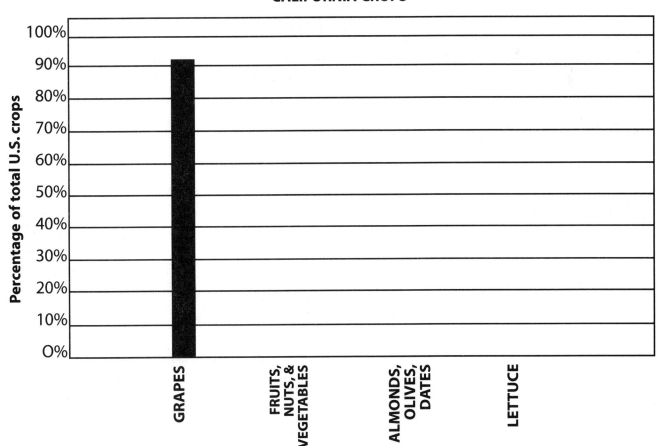

Sir Francis Drake

Sir Francis Drake was an English explorer. He became famous for his CIRCUMNAVIGATION of the earth. During his trip around the world, he sailed along the California coast. He made a LANDFALL and met with the Miwok Indians. He wanted to claim the land for his SOVEREIGN Queen Elizabeth. To mark his claim, he nailed a brass plaque INSCRIBED with the words "Great Albion." That plaque was found in 1937, ENCRUSTED with dirt and muck.

See if you can figure out the meanings of these words from the story above.

1. circumnavigation:_____
2. landfall:_____
3. sovereign:_____
4. inscribed:_____
5. encrusted:_____

Now check your answers in a dictionary. How close did you get?

Home Grown Avocados

Avocados, with their thick, green skin and scrumptous center, have long been enjoyed by many Californians. Used in salads, sauces, dips, etc., avocados add just the right flavor to many dishes. Carpinteria, near Santa Barbara, even holds a festival in the fruit's honor in October.

Just for fun, try experimenting with avocados!
You will need: 1 large avocado
                   3 toothpicks
                   1 glass of water

Insert the three toothpicks in the avocado so that only the bottom rests in the glass of water. Place the avocado in a window or other sunshine friendly location. Make a chart to check the progress of your avocado. Look in the glass. Do you see anything happening on day 1? Day 5? Write down what you see each week for a month.

Independence Day

We celebrate America's birthday on July 4. We call the fourth of July Independence Day because this is the day America declared its independence from England.

Circle the things you might enjoy on this special holiday.

Pretend you are signing the Declaration of Independence.

Write your signature here.

You can make it fancy!

Declaration of Independence

_____

What in the World?

A hemisphere is one-half of a sphere (globe) created by the prime meridian or equator. Every place in the world is in two hemispheres (Northern or Southern and Eastern or Western). The equator is an imaginary line that runs around the world from left to right and divides the globe into the Northern Hemisphere and Southern Hemisphere. California is in the Northern Hemisphere.

The prime meridian is an imaginary line that runs around the world from top to bottom and divides the globe into the Eastern Hemisphere and Western Hemisphere. California is in the Western Hemisphere.

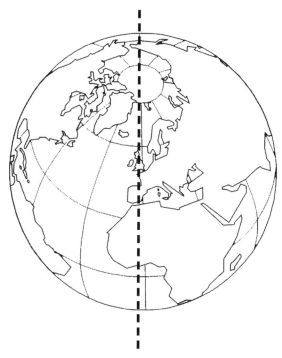

Label the Eastern and Western Hemispheres.

Write PM on the prime meridian.

Color the map.

Label the Northern and Southern Hemispheres.

Write E on the equator.

Color the map.

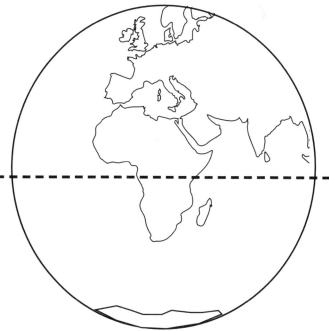

Color Me!

BROWN
Like the Grizzly Bear
Brown

BLUE
Like the Pacific Ocean
Blue

YELLOW
Like the California sunshine
Yellow

RED
Like California strawberries
Red

BLACK
Like the La Brea Tar Pits
Black

PURPLE
Like California wildflowers
Purple

GREEN
Like the national forests
Green

ORANGE
Like the Golden Poppy
Orange

CALIFORNIA

Key to a Map!

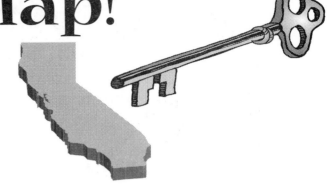

A map key, also called a map legend, shows symbols which represent different things on a map.

Match each word with a symbol for things found in the state of California.

airport

church

mountains

railroad

river

road

school

state capital

wildlife preserve

military park

Monterey Bay!

Monterey Bay in northern California has all types of Pacific marine life and beautiful and unique sea creatures. These include whales, starfish, seals, octopi, rays, kelp, and more.

Draw some other underwater friends in the Monterey Bay Aquarium.

What Do They Eat?
California Food Trivia

California food has its own distinct character and flavor with Mexican influence from the south and Asian influence from the west. Below are some foods that Californians enjoy!

Match the food with its definition.

1. Monterey jack ____
2. sourdough ____
3. gazpacho ____
4. quesadilla ____
5. guacamole ____
6. tofu loaf ____

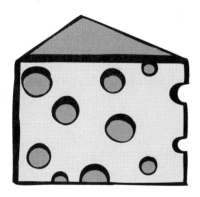

A. cheese-filled tortilla
B. dip made with mashed, flavored avocado
C. cool soup made with lots of tomatoes
D. cheese named for old California capital
E. delicious bread developed in California
F. a meatless dish made from bean curd

How many did you get right?

Are you hungry now?

Let's eat!

ANSWERS: 1.D 2.E 3.C 4.A 5.B 6.F

Legal California

California's government has three branches: legislative, executive, and judicial. The head of the executive branch is the governor. Members of the state legislative branch are either in the assembly or the state senate. Changes made to the Constitution are called amendments. The change must be ratified before it can become law. Some changes, called propositions, are put before the public in general elections. In 1920, the Nineteenth Amendment became the law of the land and gave women throughout the United States the right to vote. Women today continue to be a major force in the election process.

MORE TO LEARN

Match each word with the phrase that best defines it.

1. amendment _____

2. ratify _____

3. Constitution _____

4. General Assembly _____

5 Governor _____

6. election _____

7. proposition _____

8. women _____

A. legislation which is voted on in a general election

B. elected head of the executive branch of state government

C. people who gained the right to vote nationally through the 19th Amendment

D. an addition to the Constitution

E. the selection, by vote, of a candidate for office

F. to give approval

G. the fundamental law of the United States that was framed in 1787 and put into effect in 1789

H. the legislature in some states of the United States

Sierra Nevada Snow Globe

In Spanish, *Sierra Nevada* means snowy mountain. These mountain tops are always covered in snow. Follow the instructions below to create your own snowy mountain!

Materials:

Several sheets of newspaper
Small water tight jar (can use baby food or jam jar)
Green acrylic paint
White acrylic paint
Small paint jar
Piece of self-hardening clay (2 to 4 oz.)
Water resistant glue
Small ornament, branch or objects for your winter scene
Distilled water
2 to 4 tablespoons of of glitter (white or silver)
Narrow red or plaid ribbon (18 inches)

Instructions:

1. Spread newspaper on your work surface.
2. Test your jar by filling it with water, screwing the lid on tight, and letting the jar sit—lid side down—for a few minutes to make sure it doesn't leak.
3. Paint the outside of the lid green. You may need 2 or 3 coats. Be sure to let the paint dry for 15 to 20 minutes between coats.
4. Place a little water-resistant glue on the inside of the jar lid and work a piece of self-hardening clay into the lid. This will form a "ground" for your snow scene.
5. Press the ornament or other objects firmly into the clay. If necessary, use a little more glue.
6. If you wish, paint the clay white to look like snow-covered ground.
7. Fill the jar to the top with distilled water. Add 2 tablespoons of glitter.
8. Carefully put on the lid and tighten it firmly. Turn the jar right side up, shake it gently, then turn it over and watch the snowfall!
9. Add a little more glitter until you have the kind of snowfall you want.
10. Tie the ribbon with a bow around the lid as a finishing touch. Enjoy! You have a lovely gift!

California Word Wheel

From the Word Wheel of California names, answer the following questions.

1. I shattered the women's 100 meter dash record in 1988. _____
2. I won the 1992 Olympic gold medal in singles skating. _____
3. I joined the LPGA Hall of Fame in 1987. _____
4. I won the 1983 Rookie of the Year award for baseball. _____
5. I won 20 Wimbledon titles during my career. _____
6. I broke the home run record in 1999. _____
7. I earned 23 world and 35 U.S. swimming records. _____
8. I won Olympic gold in volleyball in 1984 and 1988 . _____
9. I skated away with Olympic gold in 1968. _____
10. I broke the "color barrier" in organized baseball. _____
11. I was voted Baseball's Greatest Living Player in a 1969 poll. _____
12. I gave golf a new image in the 1990's. _____

ANSWERS: 1. Florence Joyner 2. Kristi Yamaguchi 3. Nancy Lopez 4. Darryl Strawberry 5. Billy Jean King 6. Mark McGwire 7. Mark Spitz 8. Karcsi Kiraly 9. Peggy Fleming 10. Jackie Robinson 11. Joe DiMaggio 12. Tiger Woods

Symbols of the United States

These are some of the symbols that remind us of America. We show these symbols honor and respect.

Color each symbol.

American Flag

Statue of Liberty

Bald Eagle

Liberty Bell

Sea Creatures

What is this scary predator lurking under the water of California's Pacific Coast? Hopefully, you didn't want to take a swim! Actually, sharks help maintain a balance in the underwater world of the Pacific Ocean. They eat injured, weak, and sick fish which helps prevent the spread of disease.

 Color these spaces brown.   **Color these spaces blue.**

 Color these spaces green.

This creature is a _____ .

California Cities

Circle Sacramento in red. It is our state's capital. The star is the map symbol for our capital.
Circle San Francisco in yellow. It is a big city with many cable cars.
Circle Los Angeles in blue. It is a busy city with many people and buildings.
Circle San Diego in brown. The famous San Diego Zoo has many animals.
Circle Death Valley in green. It is one of the hottest and driest places on earth.

Oops! The compass rose is missing its cardinal directions.

Write N S E W on the compass rose.

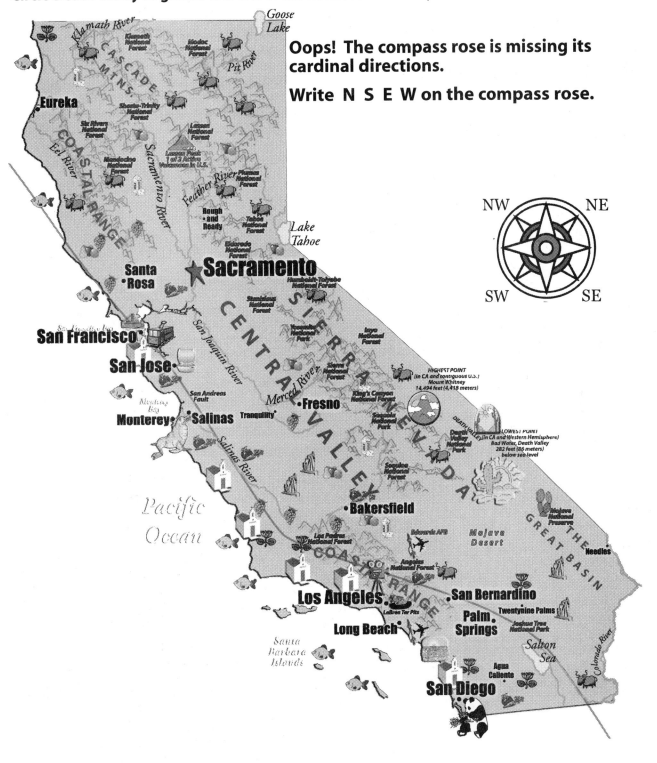

The Bald Eagle Riddle

The bald eagle is a national symbol of the United States.

Color Me!

Read the riddle and name each part of the bald eagle using words from the Word Bank.

I keep the eagle warm and dry. I am brown on the eagle's body and wings. I am white on the eagle's head and tail.
What am I?_____

I help the eagle stand and wade in shallow water to catch fish as they swim past.
What am I?_____

I am the eagle's home. Sometimes I measure 12 feet across!
What am I?_____

I help the eagle fly high into the sky. I measure 7 to 8 feet across.
What am I? _____

I am yellow. I help the eagle catch and eat fish.
What am I?_____

WORD BANK

nest   wings   bill
feet   feathers

ANSWERS: feathers, feet, nest, wings, bill

The Golden State

Good spelling is a good habit. Study the words on the left side of the page. Then fold the page in half and "take a spelling test" on the right side. Have a buddy read the words aloud to you. When done, unfold the page and check your spelling. Keep your score. GOOD LUCK!

Sacramento	1. _____
San Diego	2. _____
Sierra Madre	3. _____
Squaw Valley	4. _____
Santa Cruz	5. _____
San Simeon	6. _____
Santa Monica	7. _____
San Ysidro	8. _____
Sonoma	9. _____
Santa Rosa	10. _____
Shasta Dam	11. _____
Sierra Nevada	12. _____
San Joaquin	13. _____
San Andreas	14. _____
	15. _____

Each item is worth 5 points. 75 is a perfect score. How many did you get right?

Digging in Death Valley!

Death Valley is a desolate wasteland at the northwest edge of the Mojave Desert. The landscape is dry and hot. The lowest point in North America is located there at Badwater which is 282 feet (86 meters) below sea level. Interestingly enough, it is less than 100 miles from the highest peak in the state, Mount Whitney, which is 14,494 feet (4,418 meters) high. Many pioneers took a shortcut through Death Valley during the days of the Gold Rush. Gold prospectors also spent many years in Death Valley searching for a "lucky strike."

Help this thirsty man find water in Death Valley.

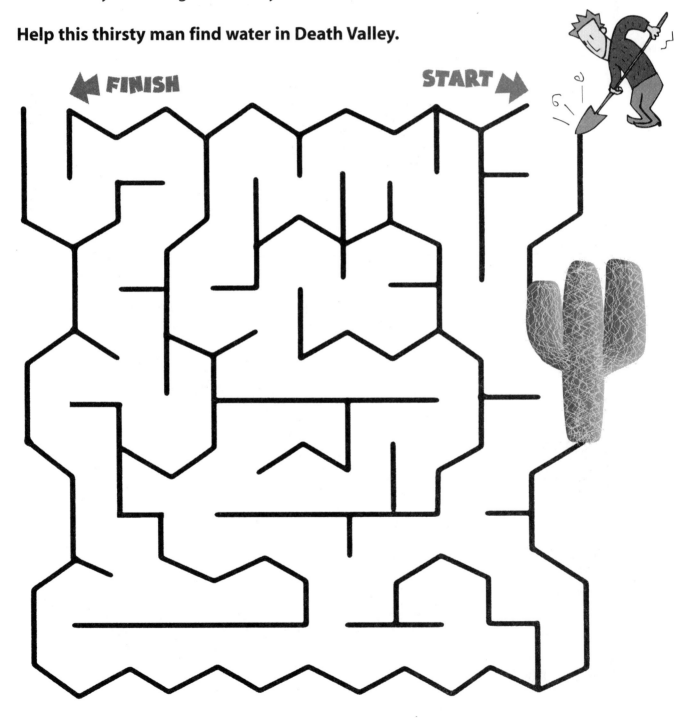

California Indians!

California's Indians lived in clans, or groups of related families. More than 100 different languages were spoken among the groups. In the southern region was the Chumash tribe. The Miwoks and Ohlones tribes lived around San Francisco, and the Modoc tribe lived to the north. It was believed that 230,000 Native Americans originally lived in the northern region.

Circle the eight things that Native Americans might have used in their everyday life.

La Brea Tar Pits!

    Several thousand years ago, around Los Angeles, oil began to ooze to the earth's surface. It became tar, and rainwater formed a pond on top of this tar. When animals came to drink the rainwater, their feet got stuck and they died because they could not escape. In 1901, geologist Bill Orcutt discovered the La Brea Tar Pits where the bones of extinct animals were preserved. Much digging took place at the tar pits and, amazingly, nearly every type of animal bone was found!

    Today, these fossil-bearing beds have become a park in Los Angeles County. If you visit this park, you can see many life-size restorations of prehistoric animals removed from the pits, including the saber-toothed cat!

Pretend you are a geologist and draw pictures of the kinds of animals you have found stuck in the tar.

Mojave Tumbleweeds

The Mojave Desert was named after a Southwestern Native American tribe. It covers a vast amount of land, roughly the same amount of land as in the states of Massachusetts, Rhode Island, and Connecticut combined! What is now the Mohave Desert was once the floor of an inland sea. It is now mostly desolate wasteland. There are many military bases located there, the most well-known being Edwards Air Force Base, where much aviation testing takes place.

Deserts are very hot and dry. Many times vegetation cannot survive. As vegetation dries up and dies, it is blown about by desert winds. Sometimes these are called "tumbleweeds." The word "arid" is often used to describe this hot, dry climate.

If you're in the mood for a delicious treat, why not try the "Mojave Tumbleweed" recipe? They go great with a glass of milk!

You will need:

1 - 8 oz. jar of peanut butter

1 - 12 oz. bag of butterscotch morsels

1 - 16 oz. can of chow mein noodles

Directions:

<u>Step 1.</u> Melt peanut butter together with butterscotch morsels.

<u>Step 2.</u> Add chow mein noodles.

<u>Step 3.</u> Drop by spoonfuls on cookie sheet and chill.

<u>Step 4.</u> Enjoy!

Our State's Rules

Use the code to complete the sentences.

A 1 B 2 C 3 D 4 E 5 F 6 G 7 H 8 I 9 J 10 K 11 L 12 M 13 N 14 O 15 P 16 Q 17 R 18 S 19 T 20

U 21 V 22 W 23 X 24 Y 25 Z 26

1. State rules are called ___ ___ ___ ___ .
   12 1 23 19

2. Laws are made in our state ___ ___ ___ ___ ___ ___ ___ .
   3 1 16 9 20 15 12

3. The leader of our state is the ___ ___ ___ ___ ___ ___ ___ ___ .
   7 15 22 5 18 14 15 18

4. We live in the state of ___ ___ ___ ___ ___ ___ ___ ___ ___ ___ .
   3 1 12 9 6 15 18 14 9 1

5. The capital of our state is ___ ___ ___ ___ ___ ___ ___ ___ ___ ___ .
   19 1 3 18 1 13 5 14 20 15

Which Famous Californian am I?

From the Word Bank, find my name and fill in the blank.

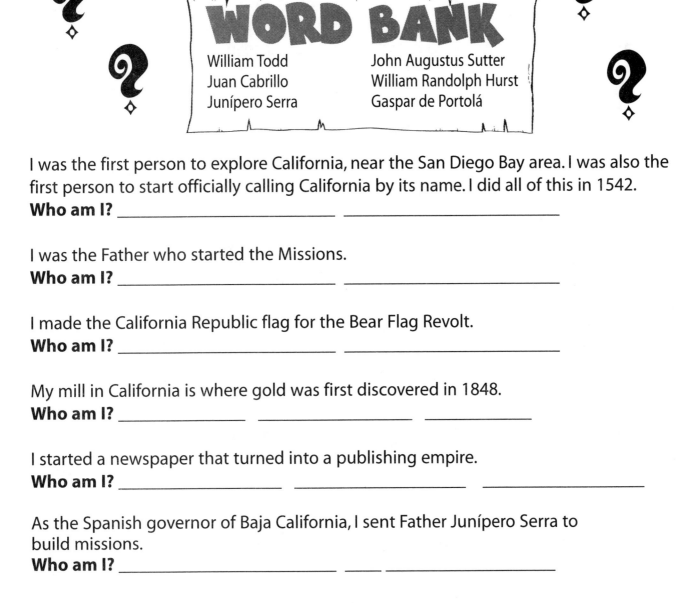

WORD BANK

William Todd
Juan Cabrillo
Junípero Serra

John Augustus Sutter
William Randolph Hurst
Gaspar de Portolá

I was the first person to explore California, near the San Diego Bay area. I was also the first person to start officially calling California by its name. I did all of this in 1542.
Who am I? _____ _____

I was the Father who started the Missions.
Who am I? _____ _____

I made the California Republic flag for the Bear Flag Revolt.
Who am I? _____ _____

My mill in California is where gold was first discovered in 1848.
Who am I? _____ _____ _____

I started a newspaper that turned into a publishing empire.
Who am I? _____ _____ _____

As the Spanish governor of Baja California, I sent Father Junípero Serra to build missions.
Who am I? _____ ____ _____

The Swallows Of Capistrano

Along the Orange Coast of California, off Ortega Highway, sits the San Juan Capistrano Mission. Founded by Father Junipero Serra in 1776, the mission is home to California's oldest building still in use, the Serra Chapel. Although this in itself is unique, what sets the mission apart from any other place in the United States is the mass of swallows that flock there each year. Returning on or near March 19 every year, the swallows take up residence at the mission until it's time for them to fly away home to South America in October.

Have you ever seen the famous swallows of Capistrano? How about other migrating birds flying high in the sky? Have you ever thought about becoming a bird watcher? California bird watching can be fun and educational!

What you will need:
Small notebook
Pen/pencil
Binoculars
Inexpensive field guide

Tips:
1. When observing birds you need to be as quiet as possible and move very slowly. Sudden movements and loud noises tend to scare birds.
2. Find something to lean against, like a tree, while you are watching the birds, so that you will be comfortable.
3. In your notebook, make notes of the sizes, shapes, colors, and sounds of the birds you see. Do their songs sound familiar? Do you notice a pattern in their flight or eating habits?
4. Look at your field guide to see if you can identify the birds you have seen.

California Weather

Because of the diverse geography of California, there is much variation in the types of weather throughout the state. From high oppressive heat in the desert— the hottest temperature recorded was 134° F (57° C)— to the frigid temperatures in the northern mountain ranges—the coldest temperature recorded was - 45° F (- 43° C). Depending on where you are, you could encounter just about anything in between! The average precipitation per year varies from as low as 5 inches per year in the Mohave Desert to over 19 inches per year in San Francisco!

The hot, dry winds, called the Santa Ana winds, begin in a high-pressure system, increase their speed, and lose moisture as they travel over the mountains to the ocean. They sometimes gain speeds of 60 mph (37.2 kph), aiding in the spread of brushfires much faster than the normal rate.

Another type of weather known in California is the "Tule fog." It happens in winter around Fresno, in the Central Valley. Named for the Native American Tule tribe, the dense fog makes traveling on the highways very treacherous.

Color the thermometer in red to show the hottest temperature recorded in California.
Color the thermometer in blue to show the coldest temperature ever recorded in California.

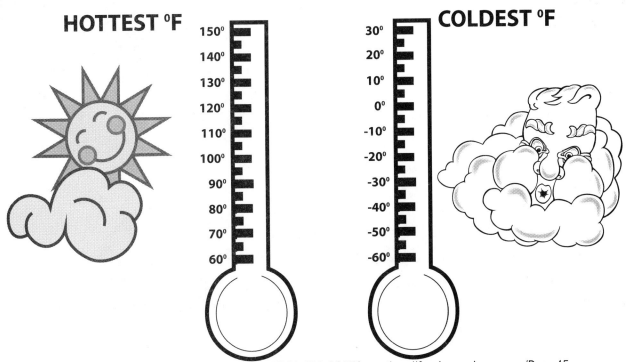

A California Harvest

Match the name of each crop or product from California with the picture of that item.

oranges _____   nuts _____   artichokes _____

fish _____   grapes _____   strawberries _____

1.

2.

3.
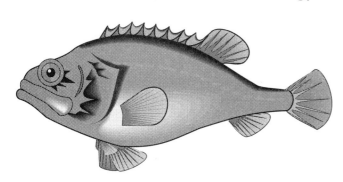

4.

5.

6.

Move to the Big City

You have lived on a farm in a small California town all your life. Your family has made the decision to move to a big city. What will you do? Where will you live? How will you get around? You write a letter to your Los Angeles friend and ask her all these questions. This is what she writes back to you:

Dear _____

_____

_____

_____

_____

_____

_____

_____

_____

_____

Bird Search!

In the Word Search below, find the names of birds commonly found in California.

HERON	ROBIN	BLUE JAY	CARDINAL
MALLARD	TEAL	WOOD DUCK	
HAWK	FINCH	KILLDEER	CHICKADEE
	HUMMINGBIRD		

```
F  R  C  B  H  I  L  M  Y  W  Q  O  C  I  P
H  T  F  A  X  M  R  Q  W  O  I  U  A  X  O
G  H  I  R  O  B  I  N  C  M  V  E  R  W  Q
X  Z  N  T  S  L  R  O  H  E  W  Q  D  J  Y
S  Q  C  G  H  U  M  M  I  N  G  B  I  R  D
F  X  H  R  E  E  O  B  C  A  Q  X  N  T  Y
S  C  H  R  O  J  E  W  K  B  V  M  A  K  O
W  R  O  Z  X  A  O  U  A  V  B  P  L  I  X
Q  O  V  M  E  Y  I  H  D  P  R  T  M  L  V
E  W  O  V  A  P  E  R  E  P  T  E  A  L  M
S  Q  P  D  M  L  P  M  E  R  P  B  M  D  Z
F  R  W  Q  D  M  L  V  C  N  O  V  P  E  X
C  V  B  N  O  U  Z  A  O  E  V  N  O  E  M
V  C  Z  O  E  H  C  O  R  M  O  Z  T  R  O
T  Y  E  Q  H  A  W  K  V  D  O  T  M  X  Y
```

Natural Disaster Area!

California is a state that is well known for its earthquakes. Did you know that the San Andreas Fault, which extends two-thirds the length of California and beyond, is the major reason for these natural disasters? Formed after shifting plates in the earth's crust collided, the San Andreas Fault marks the division of these plates. Since the plates are continuously grinding against each other, the friction between the two result in earthquakes and mudslides.

In the Word Search below, find the names of these California natural disasters.

FLOODS
MUDSLIDES
EARTHQUAKES
HURRICANES
BRUSHFIRES

```
B C R M U D S L I D E S
R H U R R I C A N E S G
U T S O R S N O U U R A
S S F L E H A D S R H L
H L R F S F C S H R S L
F M E S L I I F F I L O
I Z S I O R R M I C I P
R Q R D O E R U E A D A
E A R T H Q U A K E S D
S D O O L F H D E E S E
```

Ollie's Orange Grove

You might know that California is famous for growing oranges. Did you know that its navel orange industry began with two budlings from the U.S. Department of Agriculture? They were delivered in 1873 to Eliza Tibbets of Riverside.

How many trees do you see in Ollie's Orange Grove?
Write your answer here: ☐

Color the orange trees.

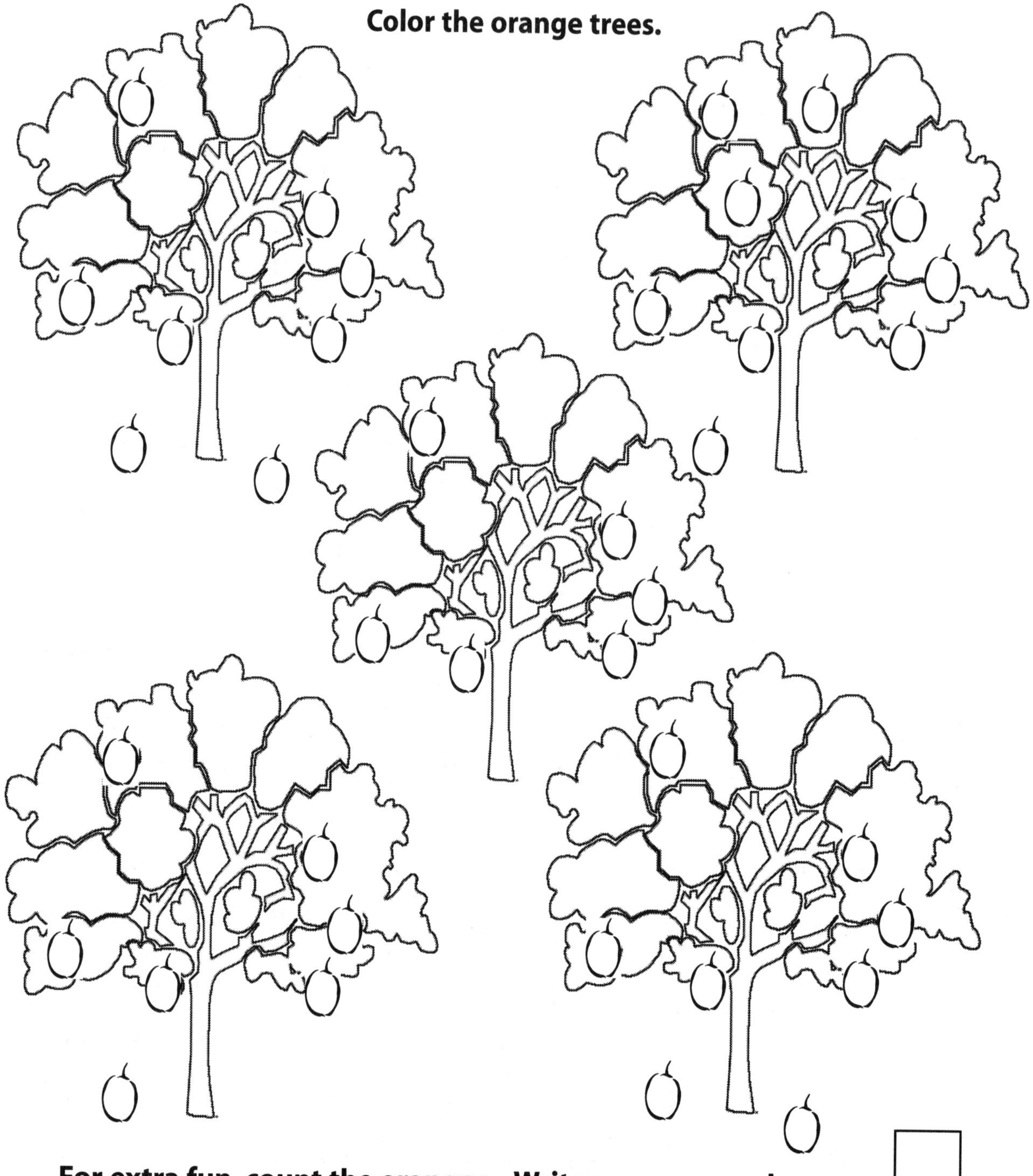

For extra fun, count the oranges. Write your answer here: ☐

ANSWERS: 5 trees, 38 oranges

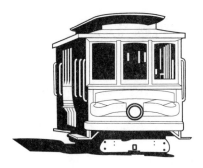

The San Francisco Treat!

San Francisco is known for its hilly, twisting streets and the cute cable cars that take people around town. First used for service in August 1873, these cable cars are recognized as the only "moving" national monument.

Let's take a spin! Hop on board and ride the historical cable car to see the Golden Gate Bridge, another of San Francisco's treats!

Hop on the cable car here and take a ride!

Sea Habitat

Why do sea animals live where they do?

Sea animals need good surroundings just like we do! California provides ample seas and a wonderful climate for its sea animals. At times, to these animals, the sea can seem like a vast bowl of soup. Often, when standing on the beach, you can see dolphins engaged in a feeding frenzy. They surface for air and dive for food. Eating is not the only thing that determines where sea animals live. Temperature, salinity, and breeding habitat all affect where sea animals live.

Put the following California sea animals in alphabetical order.

_____ skate

_____ tarpon

_____ eel

_____ squid

_____ turtle

_____ dolphin

_____ shark

_____ ray

_____ tuna

_____ blue marlin

ANSWERS: 1. blue marlin 2. dolphin 3. eel 4. ray 5. shark 6. skate 7. squid 8. tarpon 9. tuna 10. turtle

Getting Ready To Vote

When you turn 18, you will be eligible to vote. Your vote counts! Many elections have been won by just a few votes. The following is a form for your personal voting information. You will need to do research to get all of the answers!

I will be eligible to vote on this date _____

I live in this Congressional District _____

I live in this State Senate District _____

I live in this State Representative District _____

I live in this voting precinct _____

The first local election I can vote in will be _____

The first state election I can vote in will be _____

The first national election I can vote in will be _____

The governor of our state is _____

One of my state senators is _____

One of my state representatives is _____

The local public office I would like to run for is _____

The state public office I would like to run for is _____

The federal public office I would like to run for is _____

Did you know our state has 40 state senators?

No, but I do know we have 80 state representatives!

California Word Search

Find the words from the Word Bank in the puzzle below.

SETTLER	DEATH VALLEY	RANCHOS
CALIFORNIA	RAILROAD	MEXICAN WAR
GOLD	SAN FRANCISCO	BEAR FLAG
GRAPES	MISSION	MEXICO
HOLLYWOOD	STANFORD	SIERRA NEVADA

```
S M T S E T T L E R K B S C H
F E R T U R K A T E S N K F O
G X P A N A B X V N A N C R L
O I S N P N C Y S I M I A L L
L C H F K C O Q D S R S L I Y
D A L O Q H T N S S U S I T W
B N Q R S O I S O M I N F T O
S W V D F S N M E X I C O E O
T A R Z M I S S I O N O R F D
I R B W I I V G R S S N N M G
S I E R R A N E V A D A I I R
R R A I L R O A D T I V A S A
B B A B E A R F L A G L S S P
C T D E A T H V A L L E Y I E
S A N F R A N C I S C O T O S
```

California Law Comes In Many Flavors!

Here is a matching activity for you to see just a few of the many kinds of law it takes to run our state. See how well you do!

If I am this, I might use what type of law?

1. Bank robber
2. Business person
3. State park
4. California
5. Hospital
6. Real estate agent
7. Corporation
8. Ship owner
9. Diplomat
10. Soldier

Many types of laws

A. Military Law
B. International Law
C. Constitutional Law
D. Medical Law
E. Maritime Law
F. Commercial Law
G. Criminal Law
H. Property Law
I. Antitrust Law
J. Environmental Law

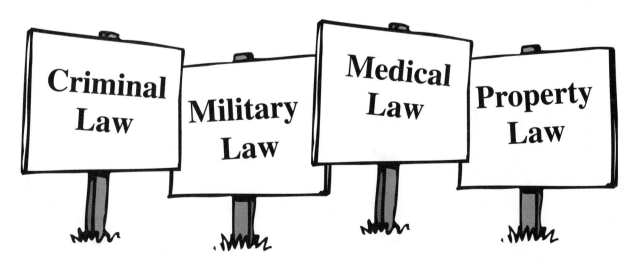

Some Patriotic Holidays

FLAG DAY

Flag Day is celebrated on June 14 to honor our flag. Our country's flag is an important symbol. It makes us proud of our country. It makes us proud to be Americans.

Count the number of stars and stripes on the flag.

_____ Stars   _____ Stripes

MEMORIAL DAY

Memorial Day is also known as Decoration Day. We remember the people who died in wars and fought so that we could be free.

Circle the things you might put on a grave on Memorial Day.

VETERANS DAY

On Veterans Day we recognize Americans who served in the armed forces.

Circle ways we celebrate Veterans Day.

Getting There From Here!

Methods of transportation have changed in California from the days of early explorers and settlers to present-day.

Match each person to the way they would travel.

Native American

race car driver

settler

astronaut

early explorer

pilot

child

Ti Yi Yippy Yay!

California cowboys lived on ranches and drove cattle on roundups. Roundups were hard work! Cattle were wild and fast. Calves were counted, and the biggest cattle were chosen to sell at market. They traveled to market in cattle drives. The trails were a thousand miles long, and cattle can only walk 15 miles a day! Trips took months and it was hot on the trail. The brims of the cowboys' hats made good umbrellas. A chuckwagon with "chow" traveled with the men. A water barrel was tied underneath. At night, for entertainment, they read and played cards or music by firelight. When the trip was over, what do you think the cowboys wanted first? If you said a bath, you are right! They went to the barber shop, and for a dollar they could soak and soak!

Color Cowboy Cody.

1. Figure how long it will take for Cowboy Cody's next trail ride if he has to go 900 miles and his cattle can only go 15miles per day.How manydays will it take?

_____

2. If there are 30 days in a month, how many months will it take Cowboy Cody to complete his trail ride?

_____

3. If Cowboy Cody started out on his cattle drive with 120 head of cattle and he lost 18 to accidents or sickness, how many did he have left to sell?

_____

Howdy, Pardner!

ANSWERS: 1. 60 days 2. 2 months 3. 102 head of cattle

California Word Wheel

Using the Word Wheel of California names, answer the following questions.

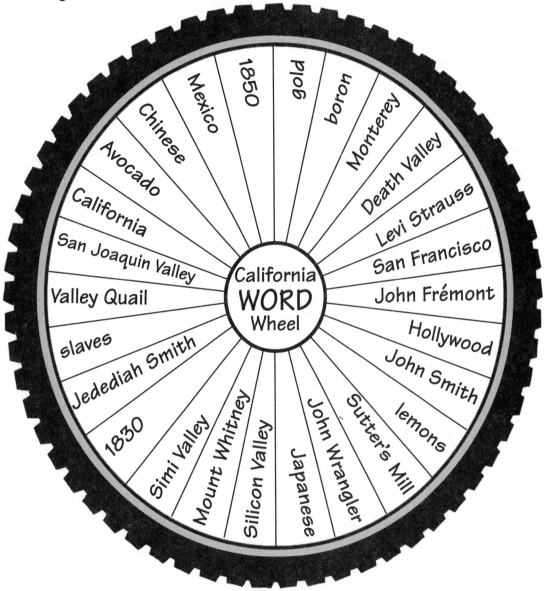

1. The fertile, agricultural land in central California is called _____ .
2. The lowest point in the U.S., located in California is _____ .
3. The highest point in the continental U.S., located in California is _____
4. California is the only state that produces this mineral: _____ .
5. Gold was first discovered at _____ in 1848.
6. In the year _____ California became an official state.
7. _____ was a famous explorer of California and one of the state's first two senators.
8. _____ was the first man to cross the Sierra Nevada mountain range.
9. _____ started a famous blue jean company in San Francisco.
10. The _____ helped build the railroads in the 1860s.

ANSWERS: 1. San Joaquin Valley 2. Death Valley 3. Mount Whitney 4. boron 5. Sutter's Mill 6. 1850 7. John Frémont 8. Jedediah Smith 9. Levi Strauss 10. Chinese

Bear Flag Revolt

During the Bear Flag Revolt of June 14, 1846, a group of American settlers revolted against Mexican rule. Raising the Bear Flag in Sonoma, settlers declared California an independent republic. The republic did not last very long. On July 7, 1846, Commander John C. Sloat of the U.S. Navy claimed California for the United States. The Bear Flag looked a lot like California's state flag today.

Design your own flag here. What do the symbols in your flag represent?

Rhymin' Riddles

Read the following riddles and try to find out which Californian they are describing.

1. Elected as President in '68, but soon I was brought down by Watergate.

   Who am I? _____ _____

2. A bad situation with the white man existed; my people and I helped out as it persisted.

   Who am I? _____ _____

3. "We need better conditions!" I vocalized. So, I helped the migrant workers unionize.

   Who am I? _____ _____ _____

4. Being born a woman was my destiny, the first in the Senate was my place to be!

   Who am I? _____ _____

5. I excelled in baseball all my life, when I broke the color barrier it brought strife.

   Who am I? _____ _____

Black Bart!

Charles Bolton (or Charles Boles) robbed stagecoaches using an unloaded shotgun! He walked to and from the crime scene, and sometimes left short poems signed "Black Bart." From 1874 to 1883, Bolton robbed 27 different stagecoaches. He never robbed drivers or passengers of their personal possessions. He only asked for the Wells-Fargo box. Read the poem he left behind.

Black Bart's Poem

I'll start out tomorrow
With another empty sack
From Wells Fargo I will borrow
But I'll never pay it back.

While reading the words of the poem, you'll notice that Bart used words that rhymed. Try writing your own verse that rhymes. Use the list of rhyming words below or think of rhyming words on your own. Remember to have a good time while you rhyme!

Rhyming Words

river	shore	sang	quiver	adore	twang
sliver	lore	bang	liver	snore	hang

_____

_____

_____

_____

_____

_____

_____

What Shall I Be When I Grow Up?

Here are just a few of the jobs that kept early Californians busy.

Lawyer	Farmer	Woodcarver
Judge	Housekeeper	Silversmith
Miner	Dairyman	Wheelwright
Teacher	Servant	Cabinetmaker
Mayor	Banker	Cooper
Carpenter	Weaver	Barber
Gardener	Telegraph Operator	Printer
Fisherman	Musician	Bookbinder
Laundress	Jeweler	Hotel Manager
Stablehand	Tailor	Minister
Baker	Pharmacist	Gaoler (jailer)
Cook	Doctor	Governor
Banker	Pony Express Deliverer	Soldier
Hunter	Blacksmith	Sailor
Beekeeper	Gunsmith	

You are a young settler trying to decide what you want to be when you grow up. Choose a career and next to it write a description of what you think you would do each day as a:

Write your career choice here!

_____

_____

Write your career choice here!

_____

_____

Write your career choice here!

_____

_____

Write your career choice here!

_____

_____

Design Your Own Diamante on California!

A *diamante* is a cool diamond-shaped poem on any subject.

You can write your very own *diamante* poem on California below by following the simple line by line directions. Give it a try!

Line 1: Write the name of your state.

Line 2: Write the names of two animals native to your state.

Line 3: Write the names of three of your state's important cities.

Line 4: Write the names of four of your state's important industries or agricultural products.

Line 5: Write the names of your state bird, state flower, and state tree.

Line 6: Write the names of two of your state's geographical features.

Line 7: Write your state's motto.

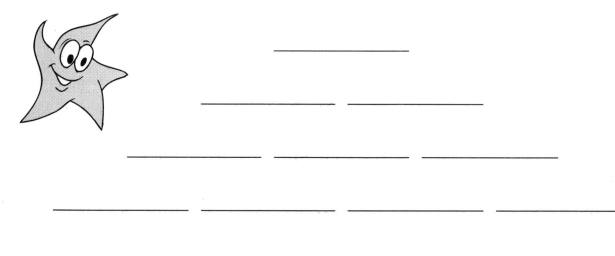

California Women of Distinction

Louise Arner Boyd led Arctic expeditions on her own chartered ships. It was the early 1900s and she was the first woman to go on such expeditions. She became so famous that a portion of Greenland is called Louise Boyd Land!

Yvonne Brathwaite Burke was the first African-American woman to serve in the California legislature when elected in 1967.

Maria de la Concepcíon was the daughter of the Spanish commander of the San Francisco Presidio. She became engaged to Russian Count Rezanov in 1857. Tragically , while he sailed to Russia to obtain permission for the marriage, he died. Maria was not aware of his death and waited years for his return. Taking the name of Mary Dominica, she became California's first native nun.

Mary Ellen Pleasant tried to take a seat on a San Francisco streetcar in 1866, and the driver ordered her to leave his vehicle, because she was black. A formidable woman, a shrewd businesswoman, Mrs. Pleasant promptly took the streetcar company to police court. From then on, declared the Capital Company, African-Americans would be allowed to ride these cars.

Julie Morgan was California's first great woman architect. She worked on Hearst Castle in San Simeon, one of the most expensive private residences ever built. The project took her 28 years!

Shirley Temple Black was a famous child star who grew up to respresent the United States in the United Nations.

How would you describe a woman of distinction? _____
_____
_____

What are some things that you do that make you a person of distinction? _____
_____
_____

Name and describe a woman you think is a person of distinction, and tell why you feel she is. _____
_____
_____

Willie L. Brown, Jr.

Willie L. Brown, Jr. was the first African-American speaker of California's state assembly. He became mayor of San Francisco in 1995. Early in his career, Brown fought racial discrimination in housing and jobs. Willie L. Brown, Jr. was a leader in the Civil Rights Movement and made a difference in California.

Many other African-Americans made significant contributions to the state of California, the nation, and in some cases, the world. Below are a few.

Try Matching these important African-Americans with their accomplishments.

_____ 1. James Beckwourth

_____ 2. Allen Allensworth

_____ 3. Yvonne B. Burke

_____ 4. Cecil Francis Poole

_____ 5. Jackie Robinson

_____ 6. Robert C. Maynard

_____ 7. Tom Bradley

_____ 8. Maya Angelou

A. first African-American to reach the rank of lieutenant colonel

B. first African-American woman to serve in the California legislature

C. broke the color-barrier in organized baseball

D. helped to create an Academy of Law Enforcement

E. mountain man who discovered the Sierra Nevada Pass in 1850

F. first African-American U.S. Attorney in the nation

G. accomplished poet who became San Francisco's first black streetcar conductor

H. first African-American to own a major metropolitan newspaper

Answers: 1.E 2.A 3.B 4.F 5.C 6.H 7.D 8.G

California Desert Tortoise

The California desert tortoise is the California state reptile. The tortoise typically lives longer than humans. It is illegal to move a desert tortoise from its native habitat.

Color the tortoise below according to the Color Key.

COLOR KEY
R = red   B = blue
Y = yellow   G = green

How many spots are on this turtle? _____

Rainbow, Pretty Rainbow

Rainbows often appear over the California countryside after a storm. Rainbows are formed when sunlight bends through raindrops. Big raindrops produce the brightest, most beautiful rainbows. You can see rainbows early or late on a rainy day when the sun is behind you.

Color the rainbow in the correct order of colors as they are listed below, starting at the top of the rainbow.

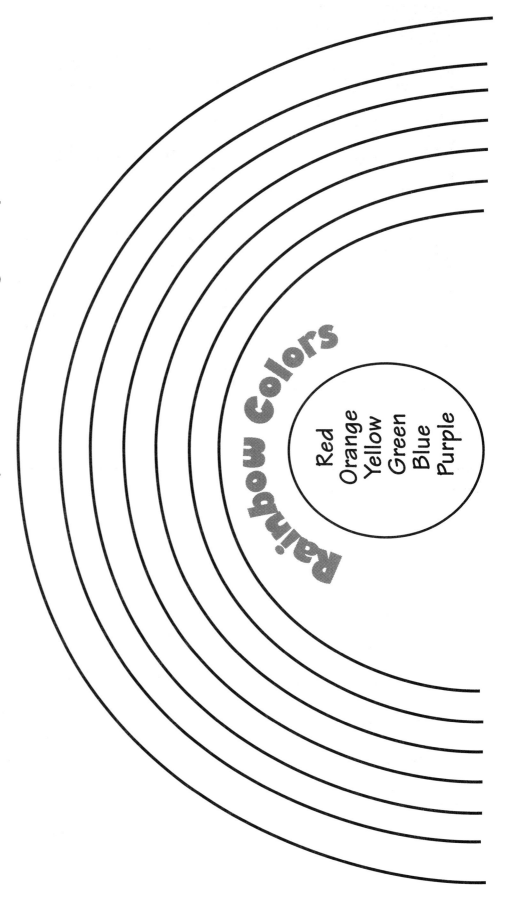

Rainbow Colors

Red
Orange
Yellow
Green
Blue
Purple

The Golden Gate Bridge

How much do you know about the Golden Gate Bridge, San Francisco's famous landmark?

Look at the statements below and decide if they are True (T) or False (F). Don't forget to check your answers!

_____ 1. The Golden Gate Bridge is located in the city of San Francisco.

_____ 2. Explorer John Frémont named the entrance to San Francisco the "Golden Gate."

_____ 3. The Golden Gate Bridge first opened in 1997.

_____ 4. The Golden Gate Bridge is the world's tallest suspension bridge.

_____ 5. The Golden Gate Bridge extends 74 feet (22 meters) above the water.

_____ 6. Over 100,000 vehicles per day travel across the bridge.

_____ 7. The Golden Gate Bridge is painted yellow.

_____ 8. It took over 5,000 gallons (18,926 liters) of paint to cover the bridge.

Answers: 1.True 2.True 3.False (1937) 4.True 5.False (745 feet, 226 meters) 6.True 7.False (orange) 8.True

The Mighty Sacramento River

California's largest river, the Sacramento, flows through the northern part of the state. It and the San Joaquin River form a delta as they wind through California's Central Valley and empty into the San Francisco Bay. This has helped to make the soil of the Central Valley rich and fertile for the farmers of California. Sitting at the intersection of the Sacramento and the American Rivers, is California's state capital, the city of Sacramento.

Use the information from the passage above to fill in the blanks below.

1. What river forms a delta with the Sacramento?

    S _ _ _   _ _ _ _ _ _ _ _

2. This river intersects with the Sacramento:

    A _ _ _ _ _ _ _ _

3. The Sacramento River has helped to make this valley fertile farmland:

    C _ _ _ _ _ _ _

4. The state capital of California:

    _ _ _ _ R _ _ _ _ _ _ _

5. The Sacramento River and the San Joaquin River empty into the San Francisco…

    _ A _

6. This group of people benefit from the Sacramento River:

    _ _ _ M _ _ _ _

7. The Sacramento River flows through this part of California:

    _ _ _ _ _ _ E _ _ _

8. The Sacramento River is in this state:

    _ _ _ _ _ _ _ _ N _ _

9. The Sacramento and the San Joaquin rivers together form this:

    _ _ _ T _

10. The largest river in California:

    _ _ _ _ _ _ _ _ _ _ O

Gold, Gold... Everywhere!

Many people rushed to California in 1849 when they found out that gold was awaiting them. Gold was first found at Sutter's Mill by James Marshall in 1848. Most of the gold found was just flakes and pieces and very seldom large nuggets. This massive movement of people immigrating to California became known as the Gold Rush. California's motto "Eureka" comes from the Gold Rush. "Eureka" is Latin for "I have found it."

Color your own treasure chest.
Woodgrain=brown,
Trim=yellow
Round Jewels=blue and green.

Fill it up with all the gold you can find!

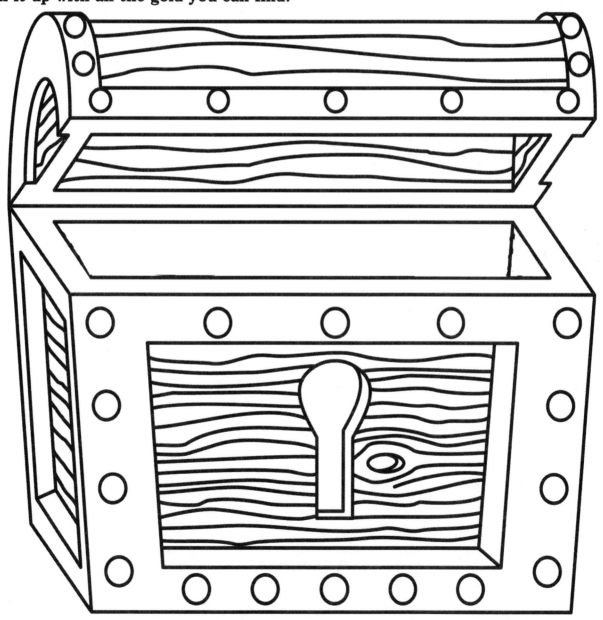

Geographic Tools

Beside each geographical "need" listed, put the initials of the tool that can best help you!

(CR) Compass Rose   (LL) Longitude and Latitude
(M) Map   (G) Grid
(K) Map key/legend

1._____ I need to find the geographic location of Germany.

2._____ I need to learn where an airport is located near San Francisco.

3._____ I need to find which way is north.

4._____ I need to chart a route from California to Oregon.

5._____ I need to find a small town on a map.

Match the items on the left with the items on the right.

1. Grid system   A. Map key or legend

2. Compass rose   B. Nevada and the Pacific Ocean

3. Longitude and latitude   C. A system of letters and numbers

4. Two of California's borders D. Imaginary lines around the earth

5. Symbols on a map   E. Shows N, S, E, and W

ANSWERS: 1.LL 2.K 3.CR 4.M 5.G 1.C 2.E 3.D 4.B 5.A

California Workers

Draw a pencil and ruler in the window for the Teacher.
Draw a cable car in the window of the Cable Car Operator.
Draw a soup tureen in the Cook's window.
Draw a Sea Otter in the window for the Marine Biologist.
Draw a saddle in the Park Ranger's window.
Draw a computer in the Computer Engineer's window.

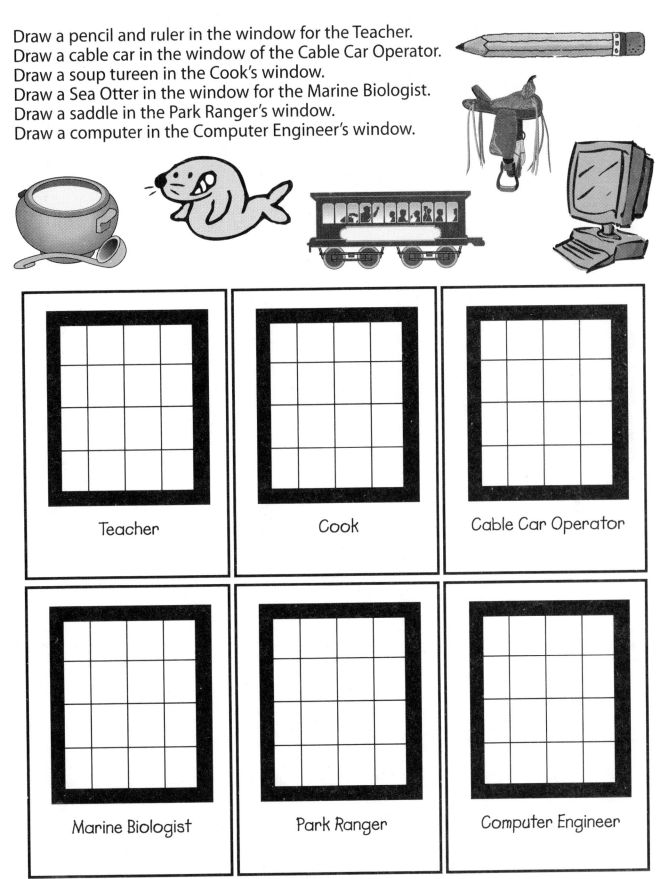

Teacher

Cook

Cable Car Operator

Marine Biologist

Park Ranger

Computer Engineer

Amazing Alcatraz

Criminals were once held in the Federal Prison on Alcatraz Island. Al Capone and Machine Gun Kelley both served time at "The Rock." Because the prison was about a mile offshore, escape was unlikely. In 1969, a Native American group called "Indians of All Tribes" claimed Alcatraz Island for themselves and some remained there until they were removed by U.S. troops in 1971.

See if you can escape from Alcatraz.

THE ROCK

San Francisco

Endangered and Threatened California

If an animal is "endangered," it means the animal's population numbers have declined to such a point that it could cease to exist. When animals reach this point they are placed on an endangered or threatened species list by the federal government. The endangered species laws were designed to protect the threatened animals and their homes. The list of endangered species for California is: San Joaquin kit fox, bald eagle, golden eagle, California condor, Northern spotted owl.

Use a resource, such as an encyclopedia, animal book, or the Internet, to find information on your state's endangered animals. Make a poster to increase awareness about this animal's threatened status. Be creative!

Example:

Save The Sea Turtle

California
Wheel of Fortune

The names of these Native American tribes contain enough consonants to play ...
Wheel of Fortune!

**See if you can figure out the Wheel of Fortune-Indian style puzzles below!
"Vanna" has given you some letters in each word to help you out!**

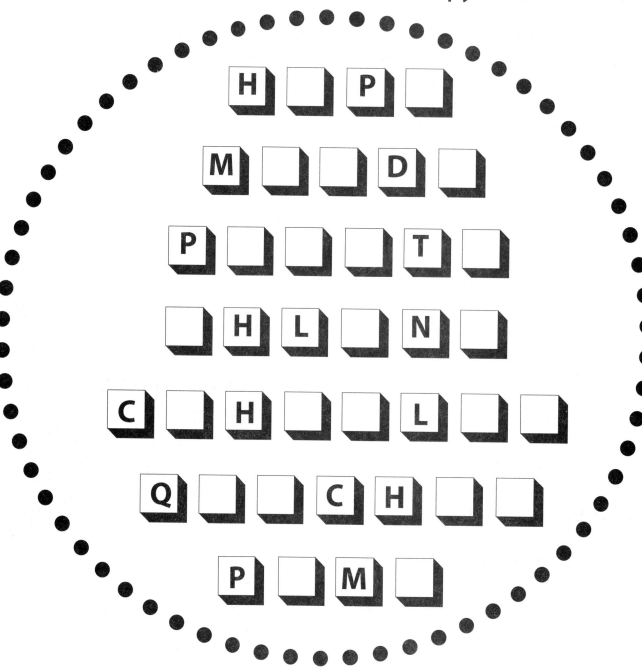

Brother Can You Spare A Dime?

After the collapse of the stock market on Wall Street in 1929, the state of California, along with the rest of the nation, plunged headfirst into the Great Depression. It was the worst economic crisis America had ever known. Banks closed and businesses crashed. There was financial ruin everywhere. In California alone, many people lost their jobs.

Our President Helps

While the nation was in the midst of the Depression, Franklin Delano Roosevelt became president. With America on the brink of economic devastation, the federal government stepped forward and hired unemployed people to build parks, bridges and roads. With this help, and other government assistance, the country began to slowly, and painfully, pull out of the Great Depression. Within the first 100 days of his office, he enacted a number of policies to help minimize the suffering of the nation's many unemployed workers. These programs were known as the NEW DEAL. The jobs helped families support themselves and improved the country's infrastructure.

Put an X next to the jobs that were part of Roosevelt's New Deal.

1. computer programmer _____

2. bridge builder _____

3. fashion model _____

4. park builder _____

5. interior designer _____

6. hospital builder _____

7. school builder _____

8. website designer _____

ANSWERS: 2, 4, 6, 7

California Authors

Fill in the missing first or last name of these famous California writers.

1. First name: Jack
   Last name: _____

2. First name: _____
   Last name: Steinbeck

3. First name: Eugene
   Last name: _____

4. First name: Robinson
   Last name: _____

5. First name: Robert
   Last name: _____

6. First name: _____
   Last name: Kerouac

7. First name: Upton
   Last name: _____

To be a reader or not to be a reader- there's only one answer!

Weather... Or Not!

What kind of climate does our state have?

- cold in the mountains
- dry and breezy in the south
- dry and hot in the desert
- The average winter temperature is about 44 degrees.
- The average summer temperature is about 75 degrees.

You might think adults talk about the weather a lot. But our state's weather is very important to us. Crops need water and sunshine. Weather can affect the tourist industry. Good weather can mean more money for our state. Bad weather can cause problems that cost money.

ACTIVITY: Do you watch the nightly news at your house? If you do, you might see the weather report. Tonight, tune in the weather report. The reporter often talks about our state's regions, cities and towns, and our neighboring states. Watching the weather report is a great way to learn about our state. It also helps you know what to wear to school tomorrow!

What is the weather outside now? Draw a picture.

People and Their Jobs!

Can you identify these people and their jobs?

Put an A by the people working at Castle Air Force Base.
Put a B by the person working at the naval district headquarters in San Diego.
Put a C by the person working at a state government job in Oakland.
Put a D by the person who mines for gold near Sacramento.
Put an E by the person working for a computer company in Silicon Valley.
Put an F by the person who works at Fisherman's Wharf.

It's Money in the Bank!!!

You spent the summer working at your uncle's manufacturing plant in Los Angeles and you made a lot of money…$500 to be exact!

Solve the following math problems.

TOTAL EARNED: $500.00

I will pay back my Mom this much for money I borrowed when I first started working (Thanks Mom!):

     subtract A ($20.00) from $500

A. $20.00

B. _____

I will give my little brother this much money for taking my phone messages while I was at work:

     subtract C ($10.00) from B

C. $10.00

D. _____

I will spend this much on a special treat or reward for myself:

     subtract E ($25.00) from D

E. $25.00

F. _____

I will save this much for college:

     subtract G ($300.00) from F

G. $300.00

H. _____

I will put this much in my new savings account so I can buy school clothes:

     subtract I ($100.00) from H

I. $100.00

J. _____

     TOTAL STILL AVAILABLE
     use answer J   _____

     TOTAL SPENT
     add A, C, and E   _____

ANSWERS: B. $480.0, **D.** $470.00 **F.** $445.00 **H.** $445.00 **J.** $145.00 TOTAL STILL AVAILABLE $45.00, TOTAL SPENT $55.00

Super Saber-toothed Cat

California's state fossil is the saber-toothed cat. Many specimens of the saber-toothed cat were preserved in Los Angeles' La Brea tar pits. Bones from other extinct species have been found at the La Brea tar pits including the mastodon, mammoth, and the ground sloth.

What do the saber-toothed cats think about the La Brea tar pits?

<u>A</u>	<u>B</u>	<u>C</u>	<u>D</u>	<u>E</u>	<u>F</u>	<u>G</u>	<u>H</u>	<u>I</u>	<u>J</u>	<u>K</u>	<u>L</u>	<u>M</u>	<u>N</u>
8	26	18	3	5	20	7	2	1	19	6	10	4	17

<u>O</u>	<u>P</u>	<u>Q</u>	<u>R</u>	<u>S</u>	<u>T</u>	<u>U</u>	<u>V</u>	<u>W</u>	<u>X</u>	<u>Y</u>	<u>Z</u>
13	22	24	9	16	11	25	15	23	12	21	14

___ ___ ___   ___ ___ ___ ___   ___ ___ ___
11   2   5   22   1   11   16   8   9   5

___ ___ ___   ___ ___ ___ ___ !
11   2   5   22   1   11   16

California Word Wheel

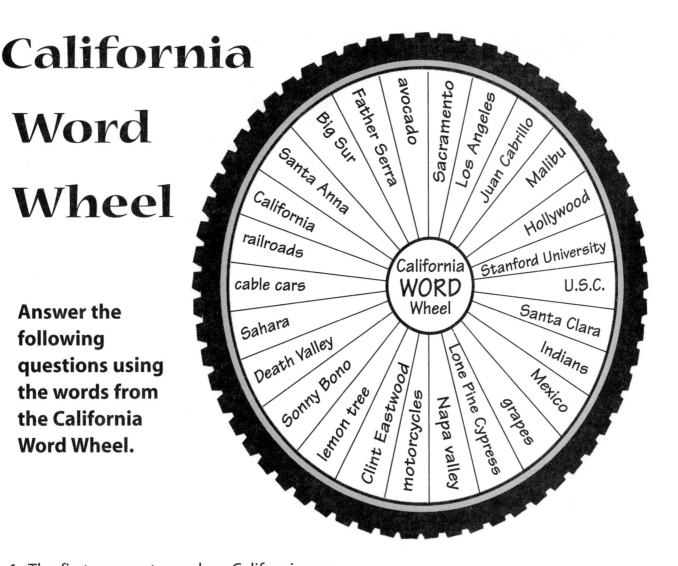

Answer the following questions using the words from the California Word Wheel.

1. The first person to explore California was _____ _____.
2. The capital of California is_____.
3. _____ _____ is 100 miles of beautiful coast.
4. _____ _____ is a large desolate desert.
5. _____ _____ is a famous actor who was mayor of Carmel, California.
6. _____ _____ is the founder of the California Missions.
7. The _____ _____ _____ is a unique tree in California.
8. _____ is home to the famous movie industry of California.
9. Leland Stanford created _____ _____ in honor of his son.
10. San Francisco has a unique type of transportation called _____ _____.

California Through the Times

Many great things have happened in California throughout its history, both past and present. Chronicle the following important California events by solving math problems to find out the years in which they happened.

1. Juan Rodríguez Cabrillo explores San Diego Bay.

    2-1=   5x1=   5-1=   6÷3=

2. Sir Francis Drake claims California for England.

    6-5=   2+3=   7x1=   3x3=

3. Junípero Serra establishes first mission at San Diego.

    5-4=   4+3=   9-3=   5+4=

4. California becomes part of Mexico.

    7-6=   4x2=   6-4=   2x1=

5. Mexico surrenders California to U.S. and gold is discovered at Sutter's Mill.

    9-8=   9-1=   2x2=   2x4=

6. Transcontinental Railroad connects California to the east.

    3-2=   1x8=   3x2=   4+5=

7. Dust Bowl immigration from Midwest begins.

    8-7=   7+2=   9÷3=   7x0=

8. Golden Gate Bridge opens.

    4-3=   4+5=   6-3=   9-2=

9. Racial riots in Watts.

    6-5=   3+6=   3x2=   4+1=

10. Earthquake strikes San Francisco.

    1+0=   8+1=   3+5=   3x3=

ANSWERS: 1. 1542 2. 1579 3. 1769 4. 1822 5. 1848 6. 1869 7. 1930 8. 1937 9. 1965 10. 1989

California State Seal

Adopted in 1849, California's seal has a grizzly bear, a miner, and Minerva, the Roman goddess of wisdom. The state motto, Eureka, also appears near the top of the seal. Eureka is a Greek word which means, "I have found it." Miners have found a lot of gold in California.

Color the state seal.

Looking For a Home!

Match the things on the left with a home on the right!

1. Runaway monkey

2. Wandering hiker

3. Computer engineer

4. Lost elephant seal

5. An excited child

6. Bighorn sheep

7. Cable car operator

8. Lost commuter

A. Disneyland

B. Silicon Valley

C. Death Valley

D. Interstate 5

E. Yosemite National Park

F. Ano Nuevo State Park

G. San Diego Zoo

H. San Francisco

ANSWERS: 1.G 2.E 3.B 4.F 5.A 6.C 7.H 8.D

Disappeared!

The California grizzly bear is the state animal, even though there are no more wild grizzlies left in the state. The last wild grizzly bear in California died in 1922. The state flag is called the Bear Flag for the grizzly bear which appears there.

Color the grizzly bear.

Circle the animal below that can no longer be found in California.

Make a Modoc Indian Vest!

Some Native Americans in California wore clothing that was made from the skins of deer and buffalo. The Modoc tribe migrated from the Great Plains where buffalo once roamed freely.

To make your deerskin vest, you will need a brown paper bag. Lay the bag flat as shown in the picture. Cut out holes for your arms and neck. Make a long slit in one side of the bag.

Ideas for decorating your vest:
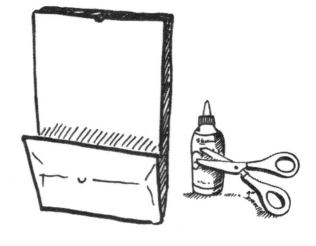
- glue buttons, glitter, and feathers on the vest

- use markers or crayons to draw Indian symbols on the vest

- make fringe at the bottom of the bag by snipping along the edges of the bag

- decorate your vest with beads, shells, etc.

Get together with your friends and have a great "pow-wow!"

Animal Scramble

Unscramble the names of the animals you might find in California.
Write the answers below the picture of each animal.

1. *rayg hwlea* Hint: This sea creature is the state marine mammal.

2. *levyla uiaql* Hint: This is California's state bird.

3. *nliacep* Hint: You will see him flying near the beach and catching fish.

4. *ase toert* Hint: He eats abalone and floats on his back in the ocean.

5. *kipchnum* Hint: She can store more than a hundred seeds in her cheeks!

How Many People in California?

STATE OF CALIFORNIA
CENSUS REPORT

Every ten years, it's time for Californians to stand up and be counted. Since 1790, the United States has conducted a **census**, or count, of each of its citizens. Practice filling out a pretend census form.

Name _____ Age ☐

Place of Birth _____

Current Address _____

Does your family own or rent where you live? _____

How long have you lived in California? _____

How many people are in your family? _____

How many females? ☐   How many males? ☐

What are their ages? _____

How many rooms are in your house? ☐

How is your home heated? _____

How many cars does your family own? ☐

How many telephones in your home? ☐

Is your home a farm? _____

Sounds pretty nosy, doesn't it? A census is very important. The information is used for all kinds of purposes, including setting budgets, zoning land, determining how many schools to build, and much more. The census helps California leaders plan for the future needs of its citizens. Hey, that's you!!

How Does Your Garden Grow?

California is the largest agricultural producer in the United States. California's diverse landscape and climate enable it to provide a variety of crops.

Can you "dig out" some of the following common California crops?

There are 22 vegetables or fruits named here.

Can you find all of them? Write the names on the lines below.

Never disparage the asparagus! Chase the scarlet runner bean! You can't beat a beet! Do you see the broccoli? Let's lumber along the cucumber. Is that a chicken in the eggplant? Here's the beginning of the endive. I give a fig for figs! Salute the London flag leek! Toss some tennis ball lettuce in the net! Are you feeling melon, cauliflower? Oh, for some okra! Walk like an Egyptian onion! May I have some May peas, please? Bully for the bullnose pepper! Cheesecake pumpkin must make good pie! The ravishing red radish is blushing! The yellow crookneck squash has warts! The very merry strawberry is giggling. A Spanish tomato is red as a cape!

_____   _____
_____   _____
_____   _____
_____   _____
_____   _____
_____   _____
_____   _____
_____   _____
_____   _____
_____   _____

ANSWERS: Asparagus, Scarlet Runner Bean, Beet, Broccoli, Long Orange Carrot, Cucumber, Eggplant, Endive, Figs, London Flag Leek, Tennis Ball Lettuce, Melon, Cauliflower, Okra, Egyptian Onion, May Peas, Bullnose Pepper, Cheesecake Pumpkin, Radish, Yellow Crookneck Squash, Strawberry, Spanish Tomato

Save the Birds!

California, with its abundance of land mass and moderate climate, is home to many varieties of birds. Along the coast, you might see pelicans, herons, geese, and seagulls. In the forest, you might catch a glimpse of owls, doves, quails, and jays. Cactus Wrens like to flutter about in the California desert. Sadly, some birds like the Bald Eagle, Golden Eagle, and the California Condor are endangered or extinct. When an animal becomes endangered, it has a chance of becoming extinct or dying off, never to be seen again. One way you can help is by becoming a friend to the birds. Begin by making a bird feeder, then sit back and enjoy their beauty as they fly in for a snack.

Materials:

1 empty, clean 1/2 gallon orange juice carton

1 pair of pointed , sharp scissors

1 wooden stick or tree limb, 10 to 12 inches long

1 large paper clip

1 bag of birdseed

1-6 inch piece of yarn or string

Instructions:

1. With sharp scissors, cut doors in the center of carton, leaving 1/2" to 1" border.
2. Cut a small 1/2" hole underneath both door frames, then slide the stick through the holes to create a perch.
3. Open the paper clip to make a hook, then make a small hole at the top of the carton and push hook through opening.
4. Add birdseed to feeder.
5. String yarn through top of hook and tie feeder to tree branch making sure it is safe from predators.

Settler Corn Husk Doll

You can make a corn husk doll similar to the dolls California settlers' children played with! Here's how:

You will need:
- corn husks (or strips of cloth)
- string
- scissors

1. Select a long piece of corn husk and fold it in half. Tie a string about one inch down from the fold to make the doll's head.

2. Roll a husk and put it between the layers of the tied husk, next to the string. Tie another string around the longer husk, just below the rolled husk. Now your doll has arms! Tie short pieces of string at the ends of the rolled husk to make the doll's hands.

3. Make your doll's waist by tying another string around the longer husk.

4. If you want your doll to have legs, cut the longer husk up the middle. Tie the two halves at the bottom to make feet.

5. Add eyes and a nose to your doll with a marker. You could use corn silk for the doll's hair.

Now you can make
a whole family
of dolls!

Please Come to California!

You have a friend who lives in Ohio. She is thinking of moving to California because she has heard that there is a lot of economic development in Silicon Valley. You want to encourage your friend to come to California.

Write her a letter describing California and some of the employment opportunities.

Silicon Valley is the home of many of the nations fastest growing companies. Many of them are high-tech companies who build or design different types of computer chips or other parts. Many jobs they offer are often also high-paying jobs.

California Banking

California banks provide essential financial services.
Some of the services that banks provide include:
- They lend money to consumers to purchase goods and services such as houses, cars, and education.
- They lend money to producers who start new businesses.
- They issue credit cards.
- They provide savings accounts and pay interest to savers.
- They provide checking accounts.

Check whether you would have more, less, or the same amount of money after each event.

1. You deposit your paycheck into your checking account. MORE LESS SAME

2. You put $1,000 in your savings account. MORE LESS SAME

3. You use your credit card to buy new school clothes. MORE LESS SAME

4. You borrow money from the bank to open a toy store. MORE LESS SAME

5. You write a check at the grocery store. MORE LESS SAME

6. You transfer money from checking to savings. MORE LESS SAME

7. You withdraw money to buy pizza. MORE LESS SAME

8. You deposit the pennies from your piggy bank. MORE LESS SAME

9. You see the interest in your savings account. MORE LESS SAME

10. You use the ATM machine to get money to buy a book. MORE LESS SAME

ANSWERS: 1. MORE 2. MORE 3. LESS 4. LESS 5. LESS 6. SAME 7. LESS 8. MORE 9. MORE 10. LESS

The Last Of His Kind

One day in 1911 a naked, malnourished Native American entered the town of Oroville. Named Ishi, the boy was the last surviving member of the Yahi Indians. This ancient Stone Age tribe was supposedly extinguished in the late 1800s. When scientists learned about Ishi, he was brought to the Museum of Anthropology at the University of California. A young researcher became friendly with him and learned about Ishi and his people's ways. Ishi actually means "man" in his native language. Ishi showed how his people built their homes, hunted with bow and arrow, and made tools. He lived the rest of his life at the museum until he died in 1916.

Help Ishi leave the wilderness to find food and shelter.

Virtual California!

Using your knowledge of California, make a website that describes different places in California. You can even draw pictures of animals, places, people, etc., to make your very own website more interesting.

John Muir

Scottish born naturalist and environmentalist John Muir was 30 years old when he came to San Francisco in 1868. After studying and exploring the Yosemite Valley, Muir fought hard to have Yosemite declared a national park. As the founder of the Sierra Club, a world-wide conservation group, Muir encouraged Presidents Grover Cleveland and Theodore Roosevelt to create a federal forest preservation system. This preserve system is now known as the United States National Forest System.

Look at the following sentences to determine if the sentences are Fact (F) or Opinion (O).

_____ 1. John Muir was born in Scotland.

_____ 2. When he arrived in San Francisco, John Muir was a very old man.

_____ 3. John Muir fought harder than anyone else to make Yosemite a national park.

_____ 4. John Muir founded the Sierra Club.

_____ 5. John Muir was foolish to plead with presidents to preserve forestland.

_____ 6. John Muir studied and explored Yosemite Valley.

_____ 7. The Yosemite Valley has the most beautiful forests in the nation.

_____ 8. The Sierra Club is a conservation group known around the world.

_____ 9. President Theodore Roosevelt helped establish a federal forest preservation system.

_____ 10. The federal forest preservation system became known as the United States National Forest System.

ANSWERS: 1. Fact 2. Opinion 3. Opinion 4. Fact 5. Opinion 6. Fact 7. Opinion 8. Fact 9. Fact 10. Fact

The Scenic Route

Imagine that you are leading a tour to famous California landmarks. Circle the following places on the map below, then number them in the order that you would visit them from north to south.

Fresno _____

LaBrea Tar Pits _____

Long Beach _____

Sacramento _____

Death Valley _____

San Francisco _____

Eureka _____

San Diego _____

Map of California showing cities including Eureka, Santa Rosa, Sacramento, San Francisco, San Jose, Monterey, Salinas, Fresno, Bakersfield, Los Angeles, Long Beach, San Bernardino, Palm Springs, San Diego, Needles, Twentynine Palms, and features including Goose Lake, Klamath River, Pit River, Lake Tahoe, Central Valley, Sierra Nevada, Coastal Range, Cascade Mtns., Mojave Desert, Great Basin, Salton Sea, Colorado River, Pacific Ocean, Death Valley.

HIGHEST POINT
(In CA and contiguous U.S.)
Mount Whitney
14,494 feet (4,418 meters)

LOWEST POINT
(In CA and Western Hemisphere)
Bad Water, Death Valley
282 feet (86 meters)
below sea level

Compass rose: N, NE, E, SE, S, SW, W, NW

All About Missions!

The Spanish governor Gaspar de Portolá of Baja, California, told Friar Junipero Serra to build missions in the new territory. Serra opened the first mission in 1769. Over the years, a chain of missions was built to the north. Missions were places where Padres, or Fathers, taught the Native Americans Christianity. However, the missions misused the Native American labor, and many fled the missions.

Help the Native American leave the mission and find his way back to the tribe.

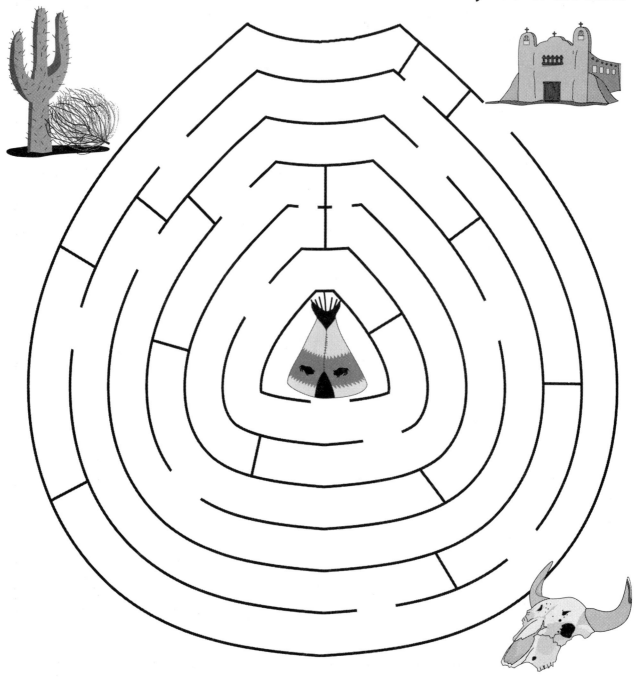

Lost at Sea!

Every year between November and May gray whales migrate along the California coast. The whales are swimming south to find warmer water for the winter.

This whale has lost his way. Help him find the other whales.

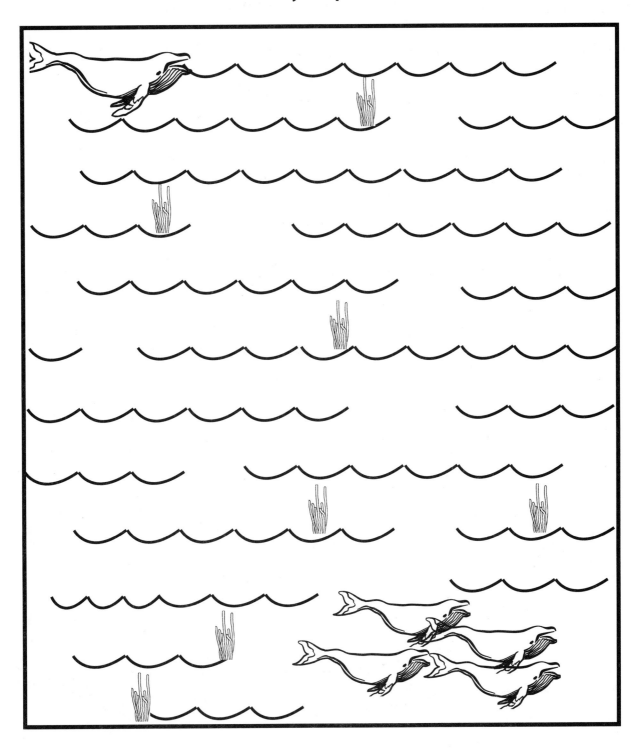

Japanese-Americans

During World War II, Japan bombed Pearl Harbor, Hawaii in 1941. This made America suspicious of Japanese-Americans because they thought they could be spies for Japan. Americans began placing Japanese in camps where they were forced to work. These camps were called internment camps.

Pretend that you were a Japanese-American in an internment camp. Write about your feelings on your imprisonment and WWII.

Flashback!

Take yourself back in time... It is 1906. You awake in a strange room you can't identify. You glance at the clock. It is 5 AM. The house is going crazy! The walls around you and the ceiling above you have taken on a life of their own. All are moving, sliding, pushing toward the other. What's that noise? Sounds of breaking glass, crashing furniture, and pounding bricks attack your senses. As you lay in bed, eyes wide with fright, the debris from the destroyed chimney goes sailing past your bedroom window. You have just lived through the devastion of the San Francisco earthquake.

Now stand up, dust yourself off, and come back to the future. Isn't it good to be home?

Match the following:

A. 1906   1. What time does the clock say? _____

B. Chimney and debris   2. What year is it? _____

C. San Francisco   3. What is happening? _____

D. Earthquake   4. Where is it happening? _____

E. 5 AM   5. What goes sailing past your window? _____

Let's Have Words!

Make as many words as you can from the letters in the words:

California, Here I Come!

_____ _____ _____

_____ _____ _____

_____ _____ _____

_____ _____ _____

_____ _____ _____

_____ _____ _____

_____ _____ _____

_____ _____ _____

_____ _____ _____

_____ _____ _____

_____ _____ _____

_____ _____ _____

_____ _____ _____

Just What Is A Redwood?

A redwood is the tallest tree on earth and can grow to heights of over 350 feet! With only two known varieties in existence today, these majestic wonders are found exclusively in California. The bark is colored a reddish-brown and thickens as it ages. Its short, droopy leaves have two layers. The top layer is deep yellowish-green in color, with the bottom layer having a more whitish appearance.

Draw and color a Redwood forest to show its natural beauty.

Famous California People Scavenger Hunt

Here is a list of just some of the famous people from our state. Go on a scavenger hunt to see if you can "capture" a fact about each one. Use an encyclopedia, almanac, or other resource you might need. Happy hunting!

FAMOUS PERSON	FAMOUS FACT
John C. Fremont	
Juan Rodriquez Cabrillo	
Barbara Boxer	
Junipero Serra	
Captain Jack	
Jacqueline Cochran	
James Marshall	
George S. Patton	
Cecil Francis Poole	
Levi Strauss	
Ronald Reagan	
Annette Abbott Adams	
Cesar Chavez	
Sir Francis Drake	
James Beckwourth	

Volatile Volcanos

Most of California was once covered with volcanic rocks. Evidence of this can be seen in Lassen Volcanic National Park. Home to Lassen Peak, it is the world's largest plug dome volcano. Still considered an active volcano, Lassen Peak's last eruption began in May 1914 and ended in 1921. Wow, that's a lot of hot air!

Sometimes nature can take us by surprise. Think of something that you have heard about or have studied concerning nature, then write a cinquain. A cinquain is a poem with only 5 lines. Look at the example below:

The 1st line has a 1 word title: Volcano

The 2nd line has 2 words describing the title: Quiet, peaceful

The 3rd line has 3 words expressing an action: Suddenly, steaming, spewing

The 4th line has 4 words expressing feeling: Scary, explosive, angry, powerful

The 5th line has a different word describing the title: Volatile

Now, write your own cinquain in the lines below:

_____

_____   _____

_____   _____   _____

_____   _____   _____   _____

_____

Political People

A state is not just towns and mountains and rivers. A state is its people! The really important people in a state are not always famous. You may know them. They may be your mom, your dad, or your teacher. The average, everyday person is the one who helps to make the state a good state. How? By working hard, by paying taxes, by voting, and by helping California children grow up to be good state citizens!

Match these California people with their accomplishments.

_____ 1. Dianne Feinstein

_____ 2. Gloria Molina

_____ 3. Adlai E. Stevenson

_____ 4. Earl Warren

_____ 5. Willie Brown

_____ 6. Yvonne B. Burke

_____ 7. Ronald Reagan

_____ 8. Mae Ella Nolan

_____ 9. Richard Nixon

_____ 10. Barbara Boxer

A. actor and U.S. president

B. first female mayor of San Francisco

C. 37th U.S. President

D. first woman to chair a committee in the House of Representatives

E. first Hispanic woman elected to state assembly

F. African-American mayor of San Francisco

G. first African-American woman in California legislature

H. first woman president of the Marin County Board of Supervisors

I. statesman and ambassador to United Nations

J. Chief Justice, U.S. Supreme Court

ANSWERS: 1.B 2.E 3.I 4.J 5.F 6.G 7.A 8.D 9.C 10.H

Gazetteer

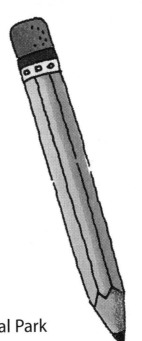

A gazetteer is a list of places. Use the word bank to complete the names of some of these famous places in our state:

1. __ __ __ __ __ __ mento

2. Point __ __ __ __ __ __ Lighthouse

3. __ __ __ __ __ Catalina Island

4. Rim of the __ __ __ __ __

5. Sierra __ __ __ __ __ __

6. __ __ __ __ Springs

7. Yose __ __ __ __ National Park

8. __ __ __ __ __ wood

9. Los __ __ __ __ __ __ __

10. __ __ __ __ __ __ Volcanic National Park

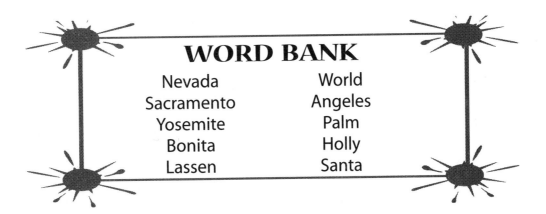

WORD BANK

Nevada	World
Sacramento	Angeles
Yosemite	Palm
Bonita	Holly
Lassen	Santa

ANSWERS: 1. Sacra 2. Bonita 3. Santa 4. World 5. Nevada 6. Palm 7. mite 8. Holly 9. Angeles 10. Lassen

Golden State Trivia
Did You Know...?

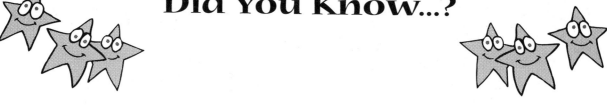

- "Mystery Spot". This is a 150-foot diameter area in the Santa Cruz mountains that no animals will go near. Redwood trees grow in corkscrews, balls roll uphill, and compasses go berserk here. It is hard for a person to stand up straight, and many have been known to faint on the spot.

- Five miles from the epicenter of 1993's huge Northridge quake, is the United States largest egg farm. Hens produce one million eggs per hour there. The amazing thing is that the quake only snapped one water line, toppled empty egg pallets, and caused only one broken egg!

- Alcatraz was known as the "escape-proof" prison. This rocky isle is located in the icy waters of San Francisco Bay. Some convicts used rafts made of raincoats to try their escape. No one knows if they ever made it.

- Fresno is both the Raisin Capital of the World and home to the bubble gum blowing champ. Susan Williams blew a 22-inch bubble and made the Guiness Book of World Records.

- Los Angeles has a wider array of ethnic markets than you will find anywhere west of the Big Apple.

- Monarch butterflies migrate from Canada by the hundreds of thousands to doze the winter away on the branches of the "butterfly trees" of Pismo Beach.

- Add another fact that you know here:_____

_____

_____

Curvy, Swervy, Lombard Street

Located in the heart of San Francisco is Russian Hill. In the middle of Russian Hill is Lombard Street, the "world's crookedest street." Known for its eight winding, treacherous curves and frighteningly steep hill, Lombard Street is a famous San Francisco landmark.

Try cycling your way through the narrow, winding curves below. You may be a bit dizzy when you finally finish!

START

FINISH

California's Geographical Features

Use the Word Bank to fill in the blanks to discover some of the highlights of California geography.

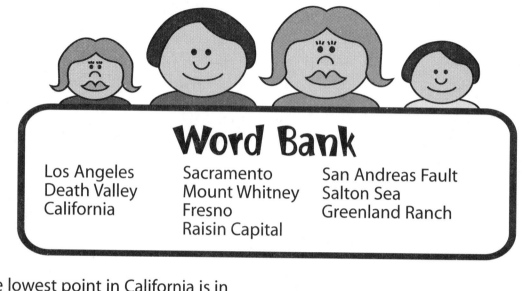

Word Bank

Los Angeles   Sacramento   San Andreas Fault
Death Valley   Mount Whitney   Salton Sea
California   Fresno   Greenland Ranch
                     Raisin Capital

1. The lowest point in California is in _ _ _ _ _ _   _ _ _ _ _ _ _ .

2. The highest point in California is _ _ _ _ _ _   _ _ _ _ _ _ _ .

3. The largest city in California is _ _ _ _   _ _ _ _ _ _ _ _ .

4. The longest river in California is the _ _ _ _ _ _ _ _ _ _ _ .

5. The 3rd largest state in the United States is _ _ _ _ _ _ _ _ _ _ .

6. The shakiest geographical feature in California is the
   _ _ _   _ _ _ _ _ _ _ _   _ _ _ _ _ _ .

7. The largest lake in California is the _ _ _ _ _ _ _   _ _ _ _ .

8. A geographical center in California is _ _ _ _ _ _ _ _ .

9. Fresno is known as the _ _ _ _ _ _ _   _ _ _ _ _ _ _ _ _ of the world.

10. A record high temperature for California was 134° F (57° C) recorded at
    _ _ _ _ _ _ _ _ _ _ _ _   _ _ _ _ _ in Death Valley.

A Trip to the Zoo!

The world famous San Diego Zoo is home to over 4,000 species of animals. Below are just a few you would see on a trip to the zoo.

Name the animals you might find at the San Diego Zoo.

_____

_____

_____

Food Festivals!

Do you have a favorite food? California has a festival for your taste buds.

Try to match each festival with its "star" food:

Orange Show, San Bernardino ____

Garlic Festival, Gilroy ____

Raisin Festival, Selma ____

Pumpkin Festival, Half Moon Bay ____

Artichoke Festival, Castroville ____

Tamale Festival, Indio ____

1.

2.

3.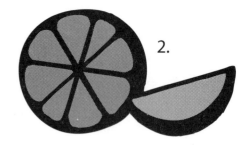

4.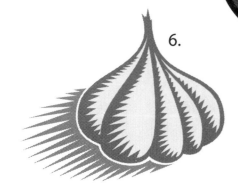

5.

6.

ANSWERS: 2, 6, 1, 5, 4, 3

The Grapes of Napa Valley

Traveling along California's Highway 29, you pass through the beautiful Napa Valley. Known for its fertile vineyards, the first winery was started in 1858 under the leadership of Charles Krug, a native of Germany. Today, many of the wineries let tourists taste their wines while they tour the wine-making facilities. Now, the grapes grown in California's Napa Valley produce some of the finest wines the world has to offer.

Using the following clues, fill in the missing letters to describe something about the Napa Valley.

1. Charles Krug came from the country of   G _ _ _ _ _ _

2. Most wineries give _____ of their facilities   _ _ _ R _

3. The Napa Valley is in this state: _ A _ _ _ _ _ _ _ _

4. Fertile vineyards that produce wine   _ _ P _ _ _ _ _ _ _ _

5. The first ____ in Napa Valley started in 1858   _ _ _ _ E _ _ _

6. Some of the finest _____ in the world come from the Napa Valley   _ _ _ _ S

ANSWERS: 1. Germany 2. tours 3. California 4. Napa Valley 5. winery 6. wines

California,
A Quilt of Many Counties

California has 58 counties.
Color the counties. Label
the name of your county
and the town where you
live.

Bio Bottles

Biography bottles are 2 or 3 liter bottles, emptied and cleaned. They are then decorated like your favorite California character. They can represent someone from the past or the present. Use your imagination!

Here are some items you may want to help you:

2 or 3 liter bottles

scissors

glue

felt

balloon or styrofoam ball for head

paint

yarn for hair

fabric for clothes

Jumping Frog Jubilee

In 1867, Mark Twain published his first book, *The Celebrated Jumping Frog of Calaveras County and Other Sketches*. Twain got his idea for the story while visiting Angel's Camp in Calaveras County. He became so fascinated when he heard people talking about a frog-jumping contest that he made it into a story.

Try your hand at writing a haiku. A haiku is a type of poem that has only three lines with a certain number of syllables in each line.

Look at the example. Then, write your haiku about something you find fascinating.

The 1st line has 5 syllables   Frogs are good jump/ers

The 2nd line has 7 syllables   Some/times they jump in con/tests

The 3rd line has 5 syllables   Do you have a frog?

Write your haiku below:

_____

_____

_____

I'm the King of Calaveras County!

Our Cities, Our Towns

California is well known for its diverse cities and towns. From Crescent City in the north to San Diego in the south, California has many interesting places to live and visit.

Match the city with something that it is known for:

1. _____ Calistoga
2. _____ Sacramento
3. _____ Coloma
4. _____ Fresno
5. _____ San Francisco
6. _____ Santa Barbara
7. _____ Hollywood
8. _____ Pasadena
9. _____ Buena Park
10. _____ San Diego

A. where James Marshall first discovered gold

B. home of the Golden Gate Bridge

C. capital of the movie industry

D. state capital

E. largest community of Hmong, a tribal people from Laos, in the nation

F. famous for its hot mineral springs

G. home of the last Spanish fort in America

H. headquarters of a world famous zoo

I. home of Knott's Berry Farm

J. where the Rose Bowl is played

ANSWERS: 1.F 2.D 3.A 4.E 5.B 6.G 7.C 8.J 9.I 10.H

You've Got Mail!

Send an e-mail to the past. E-mail a boy or girl from early California and tell them what they are missing in today's world.

WRITE	SAVE	SEND	DELETE	INTERNET NEWS AND NOTES

Who knows? You may even get a message in return... a message written on parchment with a quill pen telling you what you are missing from a simpler time!

The Golden Poppy

At the request of the Society of Colonial Dames in California, the Golden Poppy became California's state flower in 1901. The Golden Poppy grows wild all over the state. Sometimes the flowers are called flame throwers.

How many California Golden Poppy blooms can you count? _____

The Trout of Many Colors!

The South Fork Golden Trout is the state fish of California. It lives in the icy cold waters of the Kern River in the High Sierra. It is a beautifully colored species of trout. Its color is golden, with a broad pink stripe running lengthwise on its body with a brighter reddish stripe underneath it. Small black spots are scattered on the dorsal and tail fins, and on its upper sides. The South Fork Golden Trout is a rather small fish, averaging about 8 inches (20 centimeters) long.

Fill in the descriptive words below using the Word Bank.

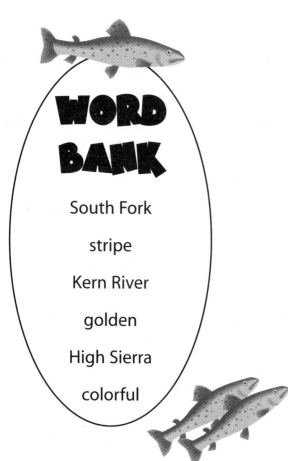

WORD BANK

South Fork

stripe

Kern River

golden

High Sierra

colorful

1. O_ _ l _ _ _ _

2. _ _ l _ _ _ _ l

3. _ _ g O _ _ _ _ r r _

4. _ _ r O _ _

5. _ _ r _ _ _ _ O r

6. _ _ _ O _ _ _ r _

Now unscramble the "bubble" letters to discover the mystery word in the sentence below:

The average length of the South Fork Golden Trout is _ _ _ _ _ inches.

Timeline

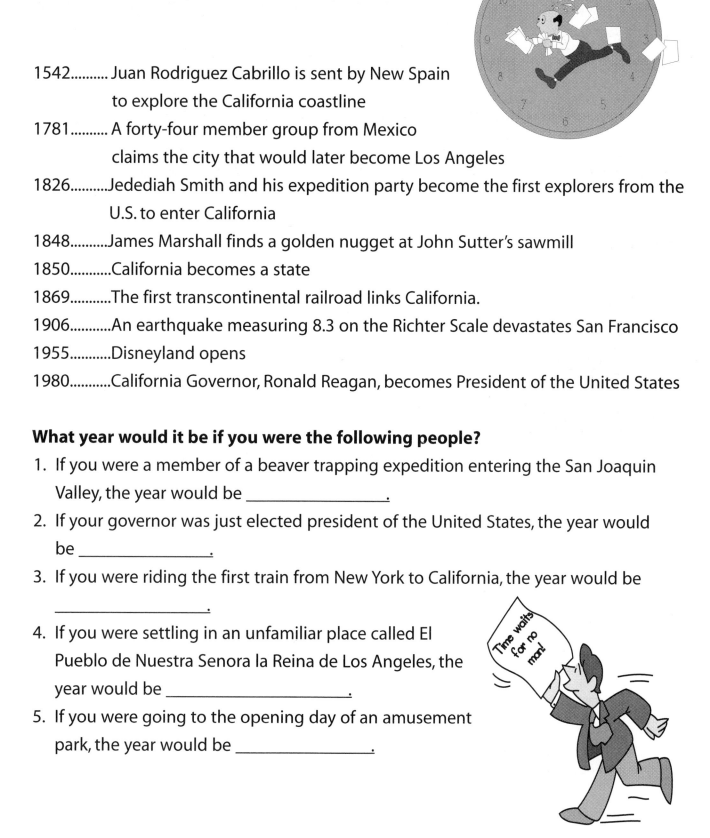

1542.......... Juan Rodriguez Cabrillo is sent by New Spain
        to explore the California coastline

1781.......... A forty-four member group from Mexico
        claims the city that would later become Los Angeles

1826..........Jedediah Smith and his expedition party become the first explorers from the
        U.S. to enter California

1848..........James Marshall finds a golden nugget at John Sutter's sawmill

1850...........California becomes a state

1869...........The first transcontinental railroad links California.

1906...........An earthquake measuring 8.3 on the Richter Scale devastates San Francisco

1955...........Disneyland opens

1980...........California Governor, Ronald Reagan, becomes President of the United States

What year would it be if you were the following people?

1. If you were a member of a beaver trapping expedition entering the San Joaquin
   Valley, the year would be _____.

2. If your governor was just elected president of the United States, the year would
   be _____.

3. If you were riding the first train from New York to California, the year would be
   _____.

4. If you were settling in an unfamiliar place called El
   Pueblo de Nuestra Senora la Reina de Los Angeles, the
   year would be _____.

5. If you were going to the opening day of an amusement
   park, the year would be _____.

ANSWER: 1.1826 2.1980 3.1869 4.1781 5.1955

Conservation in California

      Water conservation is an important issue facing Californians today. Having enough water for all of California is a problem. Southern and central California are drier than the northern part of the state. Rivers can often flood in the winter and spring. There are many programs in California that try to conserve water. The Central Valley Project is a system of dams, reservoirs, and irrigation canals that help control floods and use the water to generate electricity. The California State Water Project tries to get enough water to people in southern California. The biggest problem is that California's population is growing faster than the water supply.

What are some ways you can help conserve water? List them below.

_____

_____

_____

_____

_____

_____

_____

_____

_____

_____

_____

Two Make One 1

See if you can figure out the two words that make up the compound word.

Write the two words on the lines below the big one.

GRAPEFRUIT

_____ _____

BUTTERFLY

_____ _____

LONGHORN

_____ _____

SONGBIRD

_____ _____

BRUSHFIRE

_____ _____

EARTHQUAKE

_____ _____

RAILROAD

_____ _____

SOUTHWEST

_____ _____

HOLLYWOOD

_____ _____

SHIPWRECK

_____ _____

NEWSPAPER

_____ _____

OUTLAWS

_____ _____

CHAMPIONSHIP

_____ _____

SEASHORE

_____ _____

SURFBOARD

_____ _____

Top Ten Cities!

Here's a list of the ten largest cities, by population, in California.

Put them in the correct order (starting with the largest as #1). There's a hint in () with each city.

Sacramento (404,168)

Anaheim (295,153)

San Jose (861,284)

Santa Ana (305,955)

Oakland (365,874)

San Francisco (745,774)

Los Angeles (3,597,556)

Long Beach (430,905)

Fresno (398,133)

San Diego (1,220,666)

1. _____

2. _____

3. _____

4. _____

5. _____

6. _____

7. _____

8. _____

9. _____

10. _____

Mystery Question:

The World's tallest suspension bridge is located in this California city.

___ ___ ___ ___ ___ ___ ___ ___ ___ ___ ___ ___ ___

Here's a hint—it is a very large city on the bay, and it also has the famous cable cars!

Golden Gate Bridge

ANSWERS: 1. Los Angeles 2. San Diego 3. San Jose 4. San Francisco 5. Long Beach 6. Sacramento 7. Fresno 8. Oakland 9. Santa Ana 10. Anaheim

MYSTERY CITY: San Francisco

State Stuff Jumbles

See if you can unscramble the words below to get the scoop on all the state symbols of California.

EARKEU ———————— STATE MOTTO

HTE GNLDOE TEATS ———————— STATE NICKNAME

RICFANALIO ORDOWED ———————— STATE TREE

EGOCDFA TTERBUFLY ———————— STATE INSECT

ZYGIZRL ABRE ———————— STATE ANIMAL

IFCIPCA YRAG AWLEH ———————— STATE MARINE MAMMAL

EINOTITBE ———————— STATE GEMSTONE

ENTESNRIPE ———————— STATE ROCK

RICFANALIO EERH I EMOC ———————— STATE SONG

CEMTSORANA ———————— STATE CAPITAL

LYALEV IQLAU ———————— STATE BIRD

ELODNG PYPOP ———————— STATE FLOWER

NODGLE TOURT ———————— STATE FISH

VITANE LODG ———————— STATE MINERAL

BARSE OHTOETD ATC ———————— STATE FOSSIL

California Butterflies

In 1929, entomologists, people who study insects, voted to pick the state insect. The dogface butterfly won.

Color the dogface butterflies.

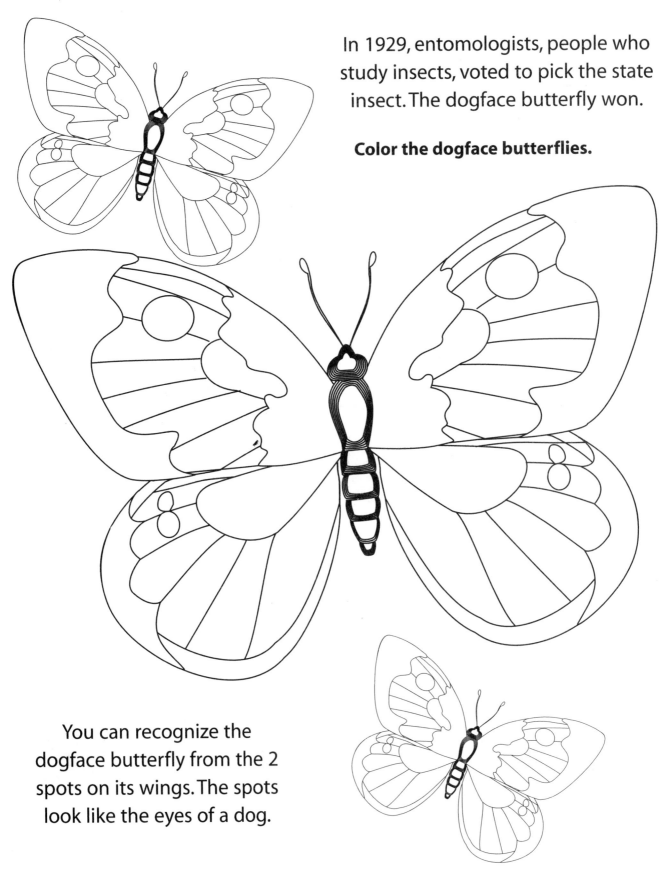

You can recognize the dogface butterfly from the 2 spots on its wings. The spots look like the eyes of a dog.